WHAT
ABOUT DOUG GILES

(AT LEAST TO HIM)

Giles's style is deliberately provocative and in your face, but it's
refreshing. Not many reverends can dish it out as well as anybody.
Giles is one of them, and even better, he's one of us.
DAVID AIKMAN
Author, *A Man of Faith: The Spiritual Journey of George W. Bush*

The Wild Man attitude is alive and well with Doug Giles and
ClashRadio.com.
CHARLIE DANIELS
Country music legend

In his unique no-compromise style, Doug Giles stands up to the
forces tearing our great nation apart, refusing to back down against
the media, political and cultural elites. Doug takes no prisoners.
JONATHAN GARTHWAITE
Editor, Townhall.com

Doug Giles's refreshing voice cuts through the moral fuzziness
of our culture with great clarity and trenchant insight. Doug's
candor, boldness and verve in tackling controversial issues make
his writings essential reading. His contagious humor provides a
delicious icing on the cake.
DAVID LIMBAUGH
Columnist and author, *Persecution*

Doug Giles is an A-team writer with a fresh and ferocious style. Doug's weekly columns on Townhall.com are must-reads.

MICHELLE MALKIN
Columnist, Fox News analyst
New York Times Best-selling author

Doug Giles and ClashRadio.com are doing a great job. Keep at it, Doug!

COLONEL OLIVER NORTH
Political Commentator

Doug Giles is the secular fundamentalist's nightmare. He has faith, hope and even a little charity. He lambastes the enemies of the Lord and of common sense. And he does it with wit as well as logic. Doug serves two great causes: religious truth and what Arnold Bennett once called "the great cause of cheering us all up."

JOHN O'SULLIVAN
Columnist and editor-at-large, *The National Interest*

Doug Giles brings a sharp, humorous, bold and captivating style to ministry.

DR. R. C. SPROUL
Distinguished theologian
Best-selling author

10 HABITS OF DECIDEDLY DEFECTIVE PEOPLE

THE SUCCESSFUL LOSER'S GUIDE TO LIFE

DOUG GILES

Regal

From Gospel Light
Ventura, California, U.S.A.

Published by Regal Books
From Gospel Light
Ventura, California, U.S.A.

Library of Congress Cataloging-in-Publication Data
Giles, Doug.
Ten habits of decidedly defective people / Doug Giles.
p. cm.
ISBN 978-0-8307-4369-8 (trade paper) ·
1. Christian youth—Religious life—Humor. I. Title.
BV4531.3.G55 2007
248.4—dc22
2007004037

1 2 3 4 5 6 7 8 9 10 / 10 09 08 07

CONTENTS

FOREWORD

Doug Giles is one of the most funny, entertaining, witty and bright commentators in America today. As a media spokesman for Young America's Foundation, I am invited to speak on many talk radio and television shows about the uphill battles facing young conservatives in academia. Without question, it is always a privilege to be a guest on Doug's radio show, *Clashradio.*

Doug's questions are engaging, his humor is priceless and his attitude is jocular—all of which facilitate a smooth, informative and captivating interview. But Doug is not just an award-winning talk radio host. He's a prolific writer and moving orator to boot! Doug's columns regularly appear on Townhall.com—one of the nation's premiere conservative websites—and he is a pastor with international reach.

Doug is a man's man. His tenor resembles John Wayne and Rambo, but his message resembles that of C. S. Lewis. He's a tough guy, both physically and intellectually. How many of us could describe ourselves as an avid big-game hunter and monster-shark fisherman in one breath, and in the next breath articulate the pitfalls of postmodernism and secular humanism? Well, Doug can.

As you'll see, Doug doesn't pull punches. Doug gives you a good laugh, makes you feel like a wuss when appropriate, and gets you on a purpose-bound track. *Ten Habits of Decidedly Defective People* is a blistering slap in the face to those who squander their talents. Doug assembles time-tested and clear ways to mess up your life and approach loser status.

Here's where Doug's hilarity and ingenuity manifest. Walk into a Barnes & Noble, Borders or even your local 7-Eleven and you'll have your pick of self-help books. A majority of these self-help books portray an inaccurate blueprint for life, usually tattering along the lines of thinking happy or positive thoughts as a way to self and spiritual actualization. Very little, if anything, is said about the importance of discipline and focus. What makes this book compelling is its contrarian approach to overcoming complacency and perpetual immaturity. *Ten Habits of Decidedly Defective People* will shame you into changing slothfulness to productivity.

Whether or not you like it, there is a war being waged on traditional values, strong work ethics and individual empowerment. This war is carried out by those who preach, *ad nauseam*, a message of victimization and dependency. That's why there is an overabundance of books that promise to bring people fulfillment in life, but never deliver on that promise.

As you read through *10 Habits of Decidedly Defective People*, you'll see that Doug is not one who just yields to this pounding. He's a fighter. He's thrown the virtues of endurance, patience and confidence back on the table. Read this book and spread the word. You are in for a real treat.

Jason Mattera
Young America's Foundation
Washington, D.C.

INTRODUCTION
FOR PERSONAL DESTRUCTION

*Human beings, almost unique in having the ability
to learn from the experience of others, are remarkable for their
apparent disinclination to do so.*

DOUGLAS ADAMS

I know what you're thinking after reading the cover. *You're thinking, Finally! It is about time someone wrote a book for me, the Decidedly Defective Person (DDP), to help me jam my face into the pavement and put whatever survives my face-plant into the meat grinder of life.*

How did I discern your inner secrets and needs?

I'm bulimic. I can read your mind.

I know. It's a trip, isn't it?

You're excited, aren't you? I feel you, man. It's crazy, ain't it? I'm ramped up as well. All the guesswork is soon going to be history from here on out for a person like you who wants to K-Fed his or her life into odious oblivion. I—and I alone—have the secrets to disastrous living. And being the benevolent guy that I am, I am going to unfold the mystery to you, the DDP. It's awesome, dude.

"What exactly are you talking about?" you ask.

Well . . . you'd better sit down, because I don't think you're ready for this jelly. Are you sitting down? All right, here we go. I'm about to unleash the beast. Hold on. The dog is nearly off the chain. Just a second. Okay, here it goes: In a little more than 140 pages, I'm going to take you to a place where there will be no limits and no boundaries for your plans of disastrous living.

Wow!

I nearly passed out just from typing that paragraph. There's power all over this room right now. The lights in my kitchen where I am typing my book on my refurbished 1996 Dell laptop are flickering on and off. Can you feel the hounds of haplessness and calamity running free within your soul? I'm getting goose bumps just thinking about how I'm going to help you make your life completely tank until you die. It's madness!

There are far too few books available today for people like you who are looking for gloomy tomes to help guide them into debt, disaster and depravity. There are only so many Sylvia Plath novels, Kafka's not writing anymore, and there is only a limited number of Jim Morrison, Jimmy Hendrix, Janis Joplin and Jerry Garcia bios out there. Once these have been perused, what's the pusillanimous slacker to do?

Books like this are what smarmy educated clods—who you don't *ever* wanna meet—call a "seminal tome," or a determining, influential book that sets the stage for revolution and change. Can you say "change"? I knew you could. And, thanks to YouTube.com, it is more than likely that the revolution of your life from bad to worse will be televised.

You will change—I guarantee it—if you follow the simple guidelines outlined in this book. All of those pipe dreams that your parents, grandparents, society, Bono and Oprah have for you will not manifest if you get zealous about what I roll out in this repository of solid waste management.

"Why would you do all of this for me?" you ask.

Good question. Well, after 15-plus years of being on the radio, writing books and columns, and speaking to a lot of people around the planet, I've been amazed at how people have both revived and ruined their lives. I have seen amazing transformations in some people as well as some astonishing self-inflicted thrashings in others.

Being the sardonic guy that I am, I'm particularly interested in those who boldly and zealously want to turn their lives into train wrecks. You've got to love them! Without them, we wouldn't feel as good about ourselves as often as we do. Yes, these folks keep *schadenfreude* alive and well, baby.

Being fascinated with the feckless has caused me to document the traits of the detrimentally determined so that I can have sure-fire bullet points for folks like you who are hell-bent for mishap. I do this because I feel it is my job to be nonjudgmental and help all people achieve their goals, whatever they may be (that's the mantra of postmodernism, isn't it?). After all, if it weren't for the losers, all of us would be lost. I mean, without the self-destroyers . . .

- There would be no *Surreal Life* or *Cops*.
- Comedies and tragic operas would cease to exist.
- The *Inquirer* would turn into a three-page positive pamphlet.
- The *American Idol* auditions would be devoid of all those Murphy's law-personified people whom we all have come to "love."
- There would be zilch to talk about at family reunions.
- Insane, steroid-abusing, career-killing NFL running backs would be a fading memory.
- There would be no more *E! True Hollywood Story* episodes about movie stars marrying and financially milking wheelchair-bound billionaire octogenarians.
- Child stars would cease to turn into ankle-biting security guards whom we get to watch simultaneously lose their fame and their sanity.
- Most columnists, radio show hosts, preachers and pundits would be officially out of work.

It is for this reason alone that I feel I wouldn't be help-ing humankind if I did not assist you, the DDP, by giving you the weapons—yeah, habits—for personal destruction. I'm here to champion people like you who do not want a purpose-driven life and who couldn't give a bleep about having a dream or a vision or personal prosperity or help-ing humankind or the planet or any other blah-blah *kum-ba-yah* crud.

> *There's nothing wrong with being shallow as*
> *long as you're insightful about it.*
> DENNIS MILLER

Now, I've got to tell you—and I hate to sound like some religious nut job here—but I really felt (sort of) for certain that it was God who was speaking to me to write to you and encourage you in your dreams, even though they are not . . . uh . . . everyone else's dreams.

"God inspired you to write this to me?" you say.

Yep, God did. The way I'm almost certain it was maybe God speaking to me is that every time He speaks to me about doing something (and it's pretty often), I begin to smell roses, gold glitter falls from the ceiling of my trailer house, and then a voice begins speaking to me in

English but with an angry and commanding high-pitched Chinese accent. It's quite an experience. Given all this, who can doubt that what I have penned for you, Mr., Mrs. and Ms. DDP, is anything *but* divine?

Anyway, enough about me. Let's get back to you.

Don't all your accomplished friends and family and the rags-to-riches folks you see on TV and in movies tick you off? They're held up and hailed as some kind of human blueprint for what we all should aspire to be. I say forget 'em. Who's to say their life trumps the mediocrity that is yours?

After all, what's so bad about your life? I mean, aside from not being able to buy a decent car, or get a credit card with a low interest rate, or move out of your mommy's house even though you are well past 30, or get anything but constantly dissed by people of the opposite sex, or earn anything above minimum wage, your life is pretty sweet.

Your mediocrity doesn't bother you. You're cool with your life. And why should you be bothered by the slings and arrows of the successful and arrogant regarding the condition of your condition?

Why does everyone try to motivate you? Your dismal job, haggard financial condition, besmirched reputation, repugnant personality and dark future don't annoy you, so why should it trouble the Tony Robbinsesizizis of this world? Besides, you've got Internet access, a wide-screen TV complete with pirated cable, a BlockBuster card and specifically chosen goofy friends who have little going for them, to comfort you. So . . . what's the big deal? If you're happy with your cruddy life, shouldn't you be left alone? Is not that what the whole "pursuit of happiness" in the Declaration of Independence is all about?

I'm with you on this one, man.

Not everyone wants a purposeful life. Not everyone wants a nice house in a good neighborhood, an excellent spouse, lovely children, a fulfilling career, positive friends and a bright tomorrow. Like art, happiness is in the eye of the beholder. And since your vision of bliss is all backward from what the GP believes is Yippee Land, I am here to help you deeply entrench your life, hopefully, into an irreparable mess.

Now, let me allay some of the initial fears you might have of not being able to completely mess up your life. More than likely, you're probably already a little squirrelly and are already pressing into Pathetic Town. Not sure this is the case? Here are five tell-tale signs to encourage you that you are well on your way to the abyss of poverty, privation and personal pain:

1. *You are constantly depressed and give up easily.* Do you get in a funk, stay in that funk and have strong desires to quit when things become tough? If so, you shouldn't sweat becoming a decidedly defective person. Sulking, brooding and getting moody and depressed when life gets difficult are essential ingredients to the loser's personal infrastructure. Laughing at trouble, getting excited when you ought to vomit and being passionately determined in the face of mounting difficulties are what characterize the butt kickers in life. If you're devoid of this internal drive and motivation, you can relax and be confident that the stage is being set for life to completely pummel you.

2. *You complain and whine all the time.* Do you complain incessantly about how tricky it is to get what life has for you? This is also an awesome trait that you, the loser, should take comfort in having. Complaining is important for several reasons. First of all, it is a great waste of precious time. Belly-aching, bemoaning and blathering on and on about your little prob-

lems eat up opportunities for action, reflection and newfound determination that will, if they attach to you, make you succeed. In addition, complaining drives the wise, positive and powerful people away from you, which is also *muy bueno* as the presence of these types of people in your life will always be a threat for success. Yes, whining will make prosperous people flee from you, leaving you alone to rot with other complainers—which is a major plus.

3. *You can't stand on your own.* Do you depend on having other people carry you through life? If so, you can take courage that you are on the right path to being slapped by the planet. Yes, looking to others, waiting on others and depending on others to make a way for you to glide into greatness are fantastic ways to ensure that you will never amount to anything. In addition, your neediness—that wake-riding trait you possess—will afford you with a plethora of excuses as to why you aren't a success in life, namely, that the people you have looked up to have let you down.

4. *You are high-maintenance and unproductive.* Do you produce very little yet require a lot of maintenance as a person? If so, take heart. Catastrophic human beings are generally fruitless in their endeavors and tend to zap the strength out of those they hang around. Therefore, if you have this trait, you can exhale because you're in the gross groove—that tame rut of incompetence and irritation that will lead you to become a real nowhere man or woman.

5. *You always miss the big picture.* Do you focus on insignificant issues and let our planet's mondo themes escape your notice? If so, here is another big reason why you should be positive about the possibilities that you will have a negative life. Yes, people who focus on minutiae never amount to anything in life. Sure, they might get a spot on TV or write for the *Inquirer* or *Cosmo,* but at the end of the day nobody respects them, and they usually die of an overdose of plastic surgery. So keep on straining at gnats, swallowing camels and obsessing on the pusillanimous and you'll prepare your soul's soil to receive the sabotaging seed from Satan. Isn't it cool?

Do you feel better now? You see, believe it or not, having a chaotic and cruddy life isn't as thorny and difficult as you might think. It is as easy as making a decision—in particular, consistently making *bad* decisions—and sticking with it no matter how much life kicks the snot out of you.

Here's a challenge: For 90 days . . . that's just *90 days* . . . commit to living out the proven loser principles outlined in this book. If you do so, I can almost promise you that you will be well on your way to . . . well . . . uh . . . to nowhere. This philosophy will work at anytime, anywhere and for anyone who desires an asinine existence.

You *can* do this. However, you must first believe that the disaster-laden life can be yours. It isn't just the acquisition of the few—you too can have a life that's a total and utter mess. Are you psyched? Well, then, let's get busy with the fundamentals. Here they are:

1. Be a slacker
2. Blame others
3. Embrace hopelessness
4. Follow others mindlessly
5. Be a self-obsessed me-monkey
6. Learn to kiss up to others
7. Be a fear-addled, backward-looking hamster
8. Quit when the going gets tough
9. Rip people off
10. Deliver less than promised

Kind of gives you the chills, doesn't it? Well, enough of my rambling, overblown, over-alliterated, oversold introduction. I don't know about you, but I'm ready to help you get busy messing up your life. What lies ahead are the fleshed-out habits for the despicable—a veritable lighthouse to channel and direct you off the Yellow Brick Road to success and keep you forever on the Highway to

Hell. And so, it is with this motive that I present you with the 10 Habits of Decidedly Defective People.

> *Courage will make you overcome danger, misfortune,*
> *fear and injustice—so forget that!*
> LURCH DREDLOCK

HABIT 1
BE A SLACKER

The tree of life is self-pruning.

JOEL DETERMAN

To solidly step away from success and to assure that your life stinks worse than a Mexican gas station toilet, you should avoid all forms of self-discipline at all cost. Yes, those who have been proficient at a putrid existence have ignored their body, mind, soul and sense of duty.

To ensure that your body conks out on you prematurely, I would focus on eating tons of fatty foods, drinking massive volumes of alcohol, chain-smoking cigarettes, getting addicted to prescription meds and making certain you seldom, if ever, get any exercise. I would make every effort to get your body so chock full of poison and so overweight that you're able to hide small toys in the folds of your fat. Excess and abuse are the keys to a sappy life. Go for it. Don't be shy. I know you can do it.

To blast past any chance of being a champion, you must focus on developing a gluttonous spirit. I'm talking about becoming so ravenous that you make Fat Albert look like a finicky and penitent Tibetan monk. Now, you're probably thinking, *How do I develop that gluttonous spirit that will help me to be the great slug I dream of being?* Well, first off you've got to idolize food, booze, cigarettes and essentially anything else that makes it hard to roll out of bed every morning.

Take food, for instance. To be an excellent slacking glut, begin to worship your groceries. Push yourself to that place where you don't just enjoy and appreciate good food and good company but actually get high from eating. This is where you want to be. Try to not care about what you eat, whom you wolf it down with or what your grub tastes like. Just focus on stuffing yourself. Yes, world-class slacking gluttons don't care about taste, health or decorum. Their concern lies only with gulping down whatever is at hand.

Being a bloated, overweight food hound will greatly assist you in your quest to be defective. Sure, you might still accomplish some things, but you will find life getting harder and harder. So take comfort and be confident in the fact that as you stuff your body full of food, you are increasing the speed at which your life will unravel.

There are several signposts to look for to make certain that you're on the right road to gluttonous ruin. These are: (1) high blood pressure, (2) a poisoned liver, (3) a bottlenose, (4) bad breath, and (5) a bulging midriff. (If you can't see your toes when you're on the scale, that's an excellent accomplishment. Go eat a gallon of cookie dough ice cream. You deserve it.)

Once you begin to see this positive stuff manifesting, you'll soon see your effectiveness quickly start going straight down the toilet. It is beautiful.

That should be enough advice regarding whacking your physical health, so now let's talk about abusing your brain. As far as your mind is concerned, I would completely blow off reading—especially reading anything substantial. Serious education is for the Einsteins of the world. And who wants to be an Einstein?

Learn as little as you can about as many things as possible.
SLAPPY WHITE

To increase the chances that the years will reek worse than a demon's armpit, embrace all forms of anti-intellectualism at all levels. According to Wikipedia, to be an anti-intellectual you've got to become hostile toward all intellectuals and all intellectual pursuits, so don't let some jerk try to get you into science, literature, world history or theology. Such knowledge could cause you to cease to be a debt-riddled and easily manipulated minimum-wage slave. Go postal, be belligerent, get vocal and attack the merits of higher education. Seek to frame yourself as an absolute simpleton. Don't let the gigantic brains of bygone days be your guide, but instead look to your guru, the *idiot emeritus*, Jethro Bodine.

As far as your life goes, if you want to be a soulless vapid waste of space, do nothing to strengthen your inner man. Let your mind, will and emotions run amok. You don't need this higher-power crud. The amazing wastoids that I have met have all been uniform in their belief that attaining a general or special revelation about God is for cripples. And you're not a cripple. You're the master of your disaster, and you're not about to allow ancient, road-tested wisdom sway your soul.

I think not, therefore . . . uh.
JIMNEY THIGPIN

The greatest losers that I have met have rarely, if ever, touched the Bible. They couldn't care less if some of the greatest and most benevolent people in history were serious believers. To develop your house of cards in the same way, convince yourself that the Old and New Testaments are unsubstantiated fairy tales written by a bunch of men a bazillion years ago and completely irrelevant for modern times.

To assure your decline in life, I would never pray, read the Scripture or even remotely follow any of its teachings. As a matter of fact, if you really want to pulverize your life, do exactly the opposite of what the Bible says. Develop a deep disdain for anything divine. This can be accomplished by implementing the following principles:

1. *Continually and habitually search for worldly amusement.* Start chasing pleasures. Fill your life with so many toys and distractions that you become completely consumed by them. I'm talking about getting eaten up with carnal things. This goes way beyond just resting and enjoying yourself from time to time—no, I'm advocating becoming a pleasure monger who is addicted to fun and allergic to godly duty.

2. *Neglect going to church for even the slightest reason.* It's raining outside, you have a slightly scratchy

throat, you stayed up all night and are too tired, the traffic is bad, your alarm didn't go off, it is your only day to rest . . . the excuse list is endless. Keep a justification file handy so that you'll have a lie ready every time you blow off attending to the affairs of your soul.

3. *When you have to go to church—like on Christmas or Easter—never participate in the church service.* Imitate a hinge whenever you're in church. Just stand there. Don't clap. Don't sing. Don't say, "Amen." Don't pray. Don't do squat. Be so immobile that they'll have to put a strobe light beside you to make you look like you're moving.

4. *Be completely disinterested in truly spiritual conversation.* Get to a place where it is easier and more engaging to talk about ridiculously in-consequential blather. Yes, gun to the place where you have either nothing to input on a conversation about God or where your depth of contribution makes Britney Spears sound like C. S. Lewis.

If you want your life to be uglier than the offspring of Quasimodo, you must also resist the impulse to commit yourself to anything. I'm talking about having an "it's not my job" mentality in all things. If you want your life to bite—and bite hard—then you've got to spread this cheese over everything you do.

To be defective, you must be a passive bystander to duty, truth and societal ills, especially if they don't directly and immediately affect you personally. I mean, why should you care about stuff that doesn't have an impact on you? It's not your job to fix what's broken, challenge what's wrong with our society or try to change what needs to be changed. You're a slacker. You're busy with more important things, like watching QVC, BET and MTV.

Y'know . . . like . . . why should you be bothered about this supposed War on Terror? You don't live in New York City or Washington, D.C., you've never been to the Middle East, and you really don't desire to go to those places. So why should you give one-tenth of a flip about this drummed-up, much-ado-about-nothing conflict? The war hasn't landed on the hood of your Toyota hybrid, so why should you care? It's not your problem and, therefore, it's not your job.

It takes 43 muscles to frown and 17 to smile, but it doesn't take any to just sit there with a dumb look on your face.
DESPAIR.COM

In addition, why should you care about the multi-billion-dollar child pornography industry? Surely it couldn't affect one of your kids . . . could it? You don't want to be one of those fanatics who are always protesting and making noise about injustices and inequities in the land. Even if you did, what can one person do? Besides, it's more than likely that your kids will never see that crud or be sexually molested by some sick individual who downloads child porn, so, like I said before, why should you get up in arms about the current 10-figure smut industry or the lenient sentences judges dole out to child rapists?

Also, lazy Christian, you shouldn't get up in arms over the systematic secularization of the United Stated. Stay focused on heaven and how some day you'll be walking around on clouds with Jesus, playing your harp in your underwear. This world's going to hell and, according to your prophecy teacher, that's the way it is supposed to be. Since any effort to remedy the situation would simply be polishing brass on a sinking ship, why should you get the least bit concerned about the current worsening of our culture?

You're not like all the misguided people out there who are trying to make a difference in this world. You know that the antichrist is coming, so your only focus is on making sure that you don't get "left behind." According to your worldview, evil triumphs over good in time and Christ only wins in eternity. It's not your job to try to change things that simply cannot be changed. That would be an exercise in futility . . . unless, of course, you're wrong.

> *Determine to be*
> *something in the world,*
> *and you will be something.*
> *"I cannot,"*
> *never accomplished anything;*
> *"I will try,"*
> *has wrought wonders.*
> JOEL HAWES

DON'T FALL FOR THIS NONSENSE!

Decidedly defective people do not have their sights set on bettering themselves. They're not looking to excel. They're just chillin'. Serious education? Please. Serious soul cultivation? That would make them some sort of religious freak. Being healthy? Whatever. Getting involved with this snafu'd planet? Forget about it.

The goal of slackers is mediocrity. They like the mundane. They're not born to be wild; they're born to be mild. They prefer ease to involvement, vacations to vocations, and ruts to ruckus. They purposely focus their attention on passivity, inactivity and indolence when it comes to anything that might demand them to move beyond what is required of them personally, professionally, ecclesiastically or culturally.

So be a *homoslackian*. Avoid self-discipline. Neglect your body and your mind. Never attempt to change anything that doesn't have a direct impact on your present condition. For when you do, you will have taken the first step in becoming a decidedly defective person.

HabIt **2**
BLAME OTHERS

*No single raindrop believes it is
to blame for the flood.*

DESPAIR.COM

For those of you who are finding it difficult to ruin your life, let me help you with 10 sure-fire ways to ram your chances of success solidly into a brick wall. Having covered the benefits of being a slacker in my last chapter, I want to continue to build on that solid foundation and further help you to pull down any chance of achievement in any aspect of your life. What lies ahead are not fluffy little feel-good debilitating ditties, but rather, secrets—yeah, keys—to developing an ineffective life.

Far from being unsubstantiated little quips for the uncommitted, these 10 habits of decidedly defective people are solid and road-tested verities for the unsuccessful. If you believe and obey them, then, like a mighty weed, failure will begin to grow and start the process of eradicating any chance for greatness in you, eventually propelling you stratospherically into the great compost heap of humanity.

Before we plow on, remember: Ruining your life is easy. Get it out of your mind that this is difficult stuff. Success is what is difficult. You have chosen that which is easy, so . . . let's get busy fleshing out your breakdown with the second habit of decidedly defective people: blame others.

Another way to assure that you never get a life is to continue to blame others for why you haven't yet accomplished anything. A must in developing a toady existence is to convince yourself that your sad lot in life is because "they, them and the other guy" have all conspired against you. Yes, you have to believe that others have wronged you and that they . . . *they* are the reason why you're a dysfunctional basket case that's never been on a date in your life.

Blame shifting is a nonnegotiable if you want to lock in misery. For those finding it hard and somewhat silly to affix blame on others, let me assist you. Try this: If you had a rough childhood—or possibly were even rejected in the womb—magnify that and milk it for everything it's worth. Use it to have people forever pity you and never expect anything from you. See how easy it is to take something other people have done to you and use it to opt out of life? (Craving perpetual pity is also a good thing to add to your jacked-up arsenal. That's a freebie!)

Think about how many miles you can get from blaming others. Throw your own pity party the next time people come around and expect something out of you. Tell them that your parents neglected you and did not pay enough attention to you and your silly antics while you were growing up because they were obsessing, as Dennis Miller has said, "on stupid things like putting food on the table and keeping a roof over your goofy head."

Yeah, that's it. Your parents disenabled you, and you hate them for not orbiting more closely to your little world. Use your parents' lack of giving you quality time as *the* reason why you lack a quality life. In fact, you know what I'd do if I were you? I'd write hate poems about them and show up at Barnes & Noble during their open mic night and skewer your parents publicly with a carpy little psycho poem about how you'd like to kill them in their sleep. That'll show 'em.

> *It's like going to confession every time I hear you speak*
> *You're makin' the most of your losin' streak.*
> THE EAGLES, "GET OVER IT"

Also, consider the possibility that your bad behavior may be caused by low blood sugar. If it is—or if you think that could even remotely be the reason—then ride that little hobbyhorse away from accountability and blame all your bad behavior on the fact that you didn't have your daily dozen sugar packs.

Another thing to think about is that if you're having a problem making money, it's probably the government's fault. Yes, ol' Uncle Sam is to blame for why you can't pay the rent on that crack house you call home. Even though everyone else is prospering in our nation (even illegal aliens!)—and prospering during the War on Terror, no less—somehow, just somehow, you're being adversely financially affected. It's got to be, got to be, the government's fault. Man, don't you hate them?

In addition to believing that your crazy lack of cash is the doing of bureaucrats in Washington, you ought to also consider the reason you're cashless is because your employers just can't see your hidden genius and your amazing talents. It's their lack of prophetic insight into your superstar qualities that is forcing you to move back home to live with your 60-year-old mommy.

Yes, whether you blame the president, myopic business owners or whoever else, the root cause of your denari deficiency certainly has nothing to do with your ridiculous absence of personal ambition, your zero creativity, your staggering stupidity or the fact that you are the biggest, whiniest and most nauseating nerve-grating pain in the butt to work with or be around.

If you don't want to do something,
one excuse is as good as another.
YIDDISH PROVERB

And please, *please*, don't allow yourself to feel bad when you see people in our country rise from poverty, debilitating setbacks, personal injuries, diseases or truly horrible familial situations to succeed in life. The way to keep this reality from freakin' you out is to renew your mind with the fact that they're just lucky. It's all about chance, not persistent hard work in a noble direction. Everyone knows that.

Are you a Christian? Well . . . you can be a big time loser as well! The under-achievers needn't be just in the secular realm . . . the saints, too, can lead a truly cruddy life. How, you might ask?

It's easy.

Fist of all, blame the devil for all your mistakes and failures. Satan is a great scapegoat for all your goofy antics. Why does the wicked one work so well as a source of blame? Well, he is evil, and we all know he tempts; so therefore he is a great candidate for culpability for all your snafus. Never mind the detail that you're such a sap that Satan wouldn't even think about wasting his personal time tempting you (he's busy working with Osama in some cave in northwest Pakistan).

The cool and convenient thing is that most Christians will buy into your noise regarding el Diablo being guilty in reference to your bedlam. Irresponsibility has become a funky bottom-line bass note for the people of God. So you need not worry about the brethren looking at you weird when you point to Old Slew Foot as the source of your *faux pas.*

The devil made me do it.
GERALDINE

Second, don't forget, Christian, that you also have at your disposal this bad ol' world to fault for all its seductive evilness. If you've overused Satan as the source of your sad lot in life, try switching off sometimes and blaming the godlessness of the unwashed world as the *raison d'être* for why you can't get off your pimpled rear.

Keep believing that the devil and the world are the primary and secondary causes for your continuous lapsing and lackluster life. What a weight off your shoulders, eh, Christian? It's society's fault and the devil's responsibility that you've been coerced to live in the wonderful world of Wussville. It's not your bad, man. It couldn't be. You're an angel.

The evil world made me do it.
DARRELL LICHT

Third (and I almost forgot this one, Mr. and Mrs. Dial Tone), you can blame your church and your pastor for not pampering your tush or coddling your little life long enough or strong enough. The church, too, is a veritable gold mine of blame—riches that will help you explain away your rancid dysfunctionalism.

Think about it.

If your minister would have paid more attention to you, or said hello more often to you, or preached more messages that would minister to you, or allocated more money from the benevolence fund toward your needs, or promoted you to a place of leadership because of your extreme spiritual giftedness and hidden character qualities, you wouldn't be out partying tonight on South Beach drinking mojitos and trying to hook up with some girl or guy. Yes, it is because of the devil, the world *and* your pastor that you are a vacant lot.

> *The Church didn't feed me enough and the pastor didn't*
> *pay me enough attention, and they made me do it.*
> MICKY BLOWSTICKY

Yes, in order to get personal mayhem maximized in the religious sphere, the Christian must never believe that he or she is remotely guilty for being a dipstick. He or she must disbelieve the plethora of biblical passages that promise victory over demonic deception or ascendancy over an acidic society. The Christian must reject the fact that responsibility for one's spiritual growth is, primarily, his or her own duty.

In my earnest attempt to help you affix failure to your funk, I want you to remember this: You can never let the thought cross your mind that you actually have a say in what happens to your life. Commit to your personal credo that you have no capability or responsibility to live by your plan and not the prescription of others.

Do not entertain the thought that you can pursue happiness. Stay away from biographies, movies, music and narratives that show people overcoming way worse crud than you have had to endure. Beware of people who have blown off what others have done to them and what others have thought of them and have, in spite of all odds, accomplished worthy goals. This could possibly empower you to quit being a weasel.

Bear in mind that accomplishment is a communicable disease that can transfer from people and can be inspired through film, music and literature. So beware whom you hang around as well as what you watch, read and listen to. You don't want greatness anywhere around you.

*Moral courage
is a virtue of higher cast
and nobler origin than physical.
It springs from a consciousness of
virtueand renders man,
in the pursuit or defense of right,
superior to fear or reproach,
opposition in contempt.*

SAMUEL GOODRICH

Finally, I need you to say this out loud, and right now: "I am a victim." "I am a casualty." "It's out of my control." There you go. Can you feel your personal power draining from you? That's good. You must declare this over and over, both out loud and in your mind, until culpability for any personal lack decisively leaves your conscience.

Also, work on a daily basis to convince your friends that you're an incurable poor dupe so that they can enable you to be more disabled. Remember: Personal power and duty are a detriment to an ineffective life, so you need to avoid any thoughts regarding liability for your life.

*I have generally found that a man who is good at man-
ufacturing excuses is good at nothing else.*

BENJAMIN FRANKLIN

HABIT **3**
EMBRACE HOPELESSNESS

*When your will is crossed and your desires are
disappointed, let that erode your faith, drown you
in doubt and sideline you forever.*

BLEEBIE BLARKA

Hopefully, you have already set in motion your destruction by digesting the first two habits and are well on your way to creating a living hell for yourself. Please tell me that you haven't become disciplined or responsible, because if you have, you're in danger of success. And that will completely mess up what we've been trying to do here.

C'mon now . . . you've got to work with me. Stay the course. Failure is just a stone's throw away. You've got to help me help you push happiness out of your life by being a doer and not just a hearer of the 10 habits of decidedly defective people.

Now, before you start sweating and freaking out about whether or not you can be unsuccessful, you must dial down and always remember that failure is easy. Since you desire to live a carefree, no-conflict, I-ain't-got-squat-going-on-in-my-life existence, these principles should go down with the greatest of ease into your inept ears and manifest rather quickly in your sickly existence. So relax . . . this is going to be almost effortless and uncomplicated.

Well, enough with this initial pep talk and my opening pleasantries. Let's continue to sabotage all your chances of prosperity and blow all probability of accomplishment to smithereens with habit #3: embrace hopelessness.

One great way to take the sizzle off your fajita is to cuddle despair. I'm talking about getting so gloomy that you make Eeyore, Vincent Van Gogh, Jackson Pollock, Ozzy Osbourne and Sylvia Plath look like Oprah on helium.

Think about it.

The bulk of the hapless people you have met in life were hopeless, right? Thus, to carve out a crevice for your life, you must stop thinking and believing that good will ever—*ever*—come your way.

Yes, hope is dangerous to your desires for failure. Reminisce a little bit about the people who have made it and you'll remember how positive and faith-filled they were no matter what difficulties they faced. Some successful people have had hope against hope.

I've seen hundreds, if not thousands, of at-risk kids, broken families and bankrupt businessmen who were up serious creeks without paddles get out of the messes they were in and dramatically turn their lives around. And what was the progenitor of their metamorphosis? You guessed it: hope. Stupid and stinking, pain in the butt, pie in the sky hope. You must beware of this encouraging force.

You said there's always worse, so technically you asked for this.
JIMMY CRACKCORN

Listen to me: Whatever it takes and whatever price you have to pay, you must purposely drain yourself of any vestige of hope if you are truly serious about courting disaster. Don't even think about getting your expectations up for positive change. If failure is what you're pursuing, hope is too promising, too provisional and too transformative to be entertained even for a moment. Hope brings faith; faith spawns an indomitable spirit; and an indomitable spirit is the precursor to the prosperity you're trying to avoid.

You must understand this or risk not moving down the dead-end road to disaster. Therefore, to evade any possible blessing, you must create an atmosphere of anxiety that will birth defeat, which in turn will crush your spirit, which will in turn ensure tragedy. And tragedy is what you want, right?

In the battle between you and the world, bet on the world.
DESPAIR.COM

One of the cool things about hopelessness is the spin-off fruit of sloth that it yields. What a beautiful thing sloth is to your debilitating battery. Classically, slothfulness was defined as the byproduct of despondency. It was not simply someone being lazy for laziness' sake, but a sign—a manifestation—that despair was ruling that person's roost, which is why he or she moved like a sea cow on psychotropes.

Yeah, as optimism is drained from your heart and mind, all your desires to get up off your butt and get busy will be snuffed. Sloth is awesome in how it extinguishes viability once you have decided to give up. Think about it: How many dejected, lazy, miserable, apathetic, depressed and passive people do you know who are full of verve (which is a must for success)? Once you embrace hopelessness, it will begin to quench all the necessary, positive attitudes and actions achievers demand and set you free to be the train wreck we all know you can be.

This book is stupid.
MARY MARGARET GILES (AUTHOR'S WIFE)

Another sweet benefit of embracing hopelessness is that it spreads to other people. Your gloominess will not only destroy your life but also the lives of all those who listen to you. Think of the possibilities! By being a hopeless wet blanket to your buddies who are too stupid to not leave you, you can be a positive influence for negativity regarding their dreams and visions.

Why is it important for you to be gracious and give your hopelessness away? Well, having given up on the pursuit of happiness, it is your duty to also try to debilitate others who are stupidly pursuing their great purpose in life. There are three main reasons for this:

1. *The potentially dangerous transference of their winning attitude spreading to you and, thereby, messing up all your chances for failure.* You have to infect them with your poisonous pessimism so that their positive attitude won't convict you for being a clod and motivate you to make meaningful change.

2. *The personal embarrassment that others' success will cause you when they leave you in the dust by actually doing something with their lives.* Think of how humiliating it would be to have others around you actually pursuing their dreams while you're still unemployed and living in your parents' basement.

3. *The jealousy and envy that will spawn in your heart over someone else's achievement will wrinkle your*

flat-line existence. And you wouldn't want that, would you? Why not? Well, you can't be happy when someone else is happy. That's why!

Therefore, it is imperative that you be the hopeless, drunken donkey that stamps on all the dreams of others.

Think about it. You've probably noticed that successful people are usually those who encourage others both in word and deed. Most players feed off the energy that they get and give to each other. Since you have decided that you're going to be a waste of space, you must determine to zap the energy out of all those around you. It is up to you to drain people of every vestige of vigor that they manifest (remember reasons 1 through 3 above!).

Your significant other is probably cheating on you right now.
RICK HOOAH

Now, before you break out in a sweat about the who, what, when, where and how of spreading your malaise, let me calm any fear that you might have about being a bad discourager. It's easy! Yielding to the voice of hopelessness and letting despair spill out of your mouth to others can be learned within a week. Please believe me that you, too, can effectively spew depressing sputum through words and body language and be an effective crippler of the creative around you. If the people you are trying to deflate do not run away from you immediately, you will, in short order, see them lay down their dreams and adopt the mediocrity that you have come to embrace.

So let's get down to the fundamentals of sharing your depression. The following tips will help you to be El Capitan of the Cold Water Bucket Brigade and enable you to grate away any chance of greatness that your friends, siblings, spouse and workmates might be entertaining. It's beautiful!

Here's how you do it. When people begin to verbalize their hopes and dreams and work toward them, immediately begin to cleverly fill up their minds with doubts and fears as to why what they're contemplating will never come true. (One caveat here: Successful people try to avoid discouragers, so be subtle. This will increase your chances of destroying another person's dreams more readily.)

Bring up all the reasons why they cannot do what they desire. Tell them that they're not smart enough, that they're going to need a lot of money, that they're not the right sex, that they're not old enough, that they're too old, that the economy is bad, that others have attempted what they're contemplating and have failed, and so forth. This technique works especially well with those who are waffling with their desires for greatness. You should see them quickly settle back into a dreary ditch, much like the one you're in.

Another wonderful passive-aggressive way to weigh people down is to always change the subject when they bring up their hopes and dreams. It doesn't matter what you change the subject to—just change it. Or go silent. Or . . . or . . . make up something right after they have unloaded their hearts and say that you've got to leave. Understand that you must only be part of a conversation when it doesn't revolve around someone getting on with life.

Now, if the people you're hanging around still see a silver lining around every cloud, suggest to them, as one comedian said, that the silver lining is the product of high levels of mercury that will eventually fall to the earth in the form of rain and slowly kill us all.

In addition, always deviously talk about being safe versus being a risk taker. Make mediocrity and the mundane look and sound appealing. Embellish your tedious and taxing life so that it appears charming. Point out people who have lost money on a risky venture or suffered setbacks, but never, ever, talk about how those people are now kicking butt and taking names while doing what they love.

Finally, if the above efforts roll off the visionaries' backs like civility off of Rosie and Donald, switch immediately to outright criticism. If the wannabe players still persist in their path, pound them with your wicked words. Bring up their past failures. Never mind that people who succeed have usually had many failures before they've finally scored.

Bring up their weaknesses in such a way that they lay trembling as they consider all of their faults and lack. Pound them with discouragement. You've got to get them to believe the worst-case scenario. Remember, it worked on you, so it'll probably work on them. Oh yeah, I almost forgot: Don't forget to gossip about them and try to poison their circle of influence. Sometimes you need the assistance of others when you're trying to clip people's wings.

Now, while trying to slay others' dreams with your words, don't forget the effective use of nonverbal communication. Roll your eyes, frown, give blank thousand-yard stares, or chuckle in a low and condescending tone. It slays 'em . . . slays 'em!

*Nobody can really guarantee
the future.
The best we can do
is size up the chances,
calculate the risks involved,
estimate our ability
to deal with them
and then make our plans
with confidence.*
HENRY FORD

One last tip to be one awesome hope-stealing wizard: Try to work your voodoo on the young. Faulty parents and jaded teachers know how well undue criticism works on their young charges. The sooner you can disparage hope in others, the better. As soon as people start showing any desire to get out of their furrows, move away from mediocrity or run from the routine, hose 'em down with doubt.

Why the need to start early with this process of discouragement? Well, most young people and green dreamers have yet to learn to defy the vision terminators. They have yet to learn that hopeless saps like yourself . . .

1. Know exactly how to achieve success . . . but are too scared or lazy to do anything about it.

2. Are fools . . . and that any fool can criticize (and most of them do).

3. Are a dissembling, contemptible race of people, and that one should view critics like a lamppost views a dog.

Be hopeless. Always look on the down side of life. And most important, be an evangelist of hopelessness so that you can keep everyone around you just as sad and miserable as you are.

HABIT 4

FOLLOW OTHERS MINDLESSLY

I think not, therefore I am not.

TWEEDLEN BALZAC

This is the fourth key in my *10 Habits of Decidedly Defective People* series. I'm praying that you are well on your way to a completely hacked-up life after just reading and obeying the first 3 of the 10 habits. However, if success is still looking like it might attach itself to you, do not despair. Stay the course and chaos *will* be yours. Be patient, as fiascos can take time and setting in motion the forces for failure demands dedication. Be vigilant and the repugnant life will be yours before you know it.

With habits 1 through 3 firmly under your belt, let me further your farcical existence by establishing within your smelly psyche habit #4: follow others mindlessly. To eschew achievement—which is your ultimate goal—you must flee from all the traits that make one great (duh). Some of the qualities that make people great are leading thoughtfully, being independent thinkers, having a well-tuned moral compass, being persons of conviction rather than convenience, and being very comfortable with opposing what others are robotically doing. Yes, the successful people got to that place of personal prosperity through self-determined deliberation, which is totally taboo for those trying to attract atrocities.

Developing the wisdom, knowledge and understanding that leads to independent thinking is hard work—and hard work is antithetical to your desires for doom. Only through sweat do the successful attain the ability to solidly think against the grain, and because you are devoted to disaster and immediate gratification, developing the powers necessary for sound judgment is simply not on your to-do list. You, you loser you, would rather take the path of least resistance and cruise on the flotsam and jetsam of a jaded culture. That's why you follow others mindlessly.

Getting thoughtlessly caught up in what others are doing is a must if you really want to rust. This is especially true for young people. If you are a young person, you must begin to immediately start obeying all that your buddies are telling you to do. Quit thinking so much. You must also cease examining what you're being sold by your peers. Quit judging their attitudes and actions, or you might be putting off some foul existence that could be yours.

> *Education is the inculcation of the incomprehensible*
> *into the indifferent by the incompetent.*
> JOHN MAYNARD KEYNES

Did you ever consider that? I mean think about it . . . if you stay true to your own thoughts and convictions, you could end up being ridiculed, persecuted or ostra-cized—or even get *blogged*! And you wouldn't want that, would you? So quit this independent crud and just con-form. Get your uniform on and walk lockstep with all the other saps in this culture.

To enable failure to ooze over your soul, you must allow your convictions to wane and your will to weaken. You must actively foster the fear of man within as it wilts your wussy soul. The opportunities to follow the herd are endless. You can become like all the other cattle at nearly every turn.

Walking on Water

One particular group of Christians attempted to follow
in Jesus' footsteps more literally than most.
They worked to master the secret of walking on water.
Diligently, day by day, the group tried to be closer to
God by making a sincere effort to walk on water. These
Christians continued their unorthodox practices until
the leader of this small Los Angeles group unexpectedly
died while practicing in his bathtub. His wife said James
spent many hours trying to perfect the technique of
walking on water, but had not yet mastered the ability.
He apparently drowned after slipping on a bar of soap.

DARWINAWARDS.COM

Take your sex life, for instance. Following what our current, cranially posterialized culture is doing is a great way to jettison your future into the fryer. I mean . . . who needs morality? Abstinence is for morons. Why give yourself to one person out of love when you can have sex with 50-plus via lust? You, my friend, should sleep around as much as possible and give free reign to all those impulses that you have.

Yes, through the avenue of multiple sexual partners, you can fragment your soul to the point where sex becomes mechanized and all semblances of love and devotion are effectively destroyed. Come on now. Kinsey your way to disaster.

Additionally, think about the pain you could be missing out on (not to mention the amazing complications) by not having an unwanted child, an abortion, an STD or even AIDS! You are missing out on so much disaster by following your holier-than-thou moral compass. Cut the conviction stuff immediately and get busy following what others are doing with their naughty bits, you repressed puritan, you. Never mind what common sense, holy writ and history have taught us about unbridled sexual passions.

Isn't there any other part of the matzo you can eat?
MARILYN MONROE, AFTER BEING SERVED MATZO BALL
SOUP THREE DAYS IN A ROW

Yes, to truly enhance your chances for hell on Earth, you have to cease to think for yourself and become enslaved to other people, TV, feckless political parties and corrupt ecclesia. Do not develop the powers of common sense. Do not study the rise and fall of nations and their worldviews. Never doubt that current thought or trends have been previously tried and found wanting. Teach yourself to be enslaved to public opinion. Live under the authoritative whip of the thought police, ever fearing man and marching to the beat of the masses' drum. Bring on disaster by thinking nothing, saying nothing, doing nothing and being nothing different than what everyone else is.

Now, if you're finding that simply following others mindlessly isn't slaying your life quickly enough, go the second mile: Don't just follow what idiots are doing, *but actually befriend the idiots.* Sometimes it's not enough to just follow others mindlessly. You and I both know that you can trail others without befriending them. However, if you really want to win at losing, you must go the distance and physically merge your life with other losers. I'm talking about palling around with them, marrying them and talking to them on a regular basis. If you're serious about living la Vida Broka, you must intentionally and strategically establish, as much as you can, blithering idiots as your closest confidants.

*It is delightful
to transport one's self
into the spirit of the past,
to see how a wise man
has thought before us,
and to what glorious height
we have last reached.*

JOHANN WOLFGANG VON GOETHE

Now, don't blow off this point like it is insignificant, because constant contact with these idiots can increase your potential for pain like nothing else can. Think about those lucky unlucky few who have already mastered disaster. Who do they run around with? Other accomplished failures, of course! Do the math.

Therefore, if you want your life to reek, you need to hang out with people who stink. Before you know it, you will be messing up immensely and life will be passing you by. Isn't that cool? And it is all made possible simply by making friends with the decrepit and having their losing spirit permeate your soul. (You owe me big money for this wisdom.)

Yes, bad company will corrupt your chances for a good life, and that's what you want, correct? You want to make sure that your chances for achievement diminish daily. Can I hear an "amen"?

If befriended, the achievers and dreamers, the disciplined and responsible, the independent and physically fit and the balanced and bold can absolutely squirrel your chances for failure. So if you meet these people, run, brother, run! Wise people beget wise people. Success births success, so be shrewd and hang out with stupid people—and stupid people only—if you want life to slap you. Comprende?

Husbands and wives, if you want to destroy your marriage (and who doesn't, right?) and cause yourself, your kids, your relatives and your friends serious pain while loading on your shoulders a massive burden that threatens your chances for success, hang out with people who take your wedding vows lightly. Find, follow and befriend those who encourage infidelity and who sow discord between you and your mate. Trust me, before long that pretty decent marriage you've got will be shattered to smithereens. Think about it: Just by hanging out with a clod, you will more than likely have buckets of misfortune, you lucky person, you.

Nowadays, you can find the feckless marital infidels to help you destroy your nuptials almost anywhere. Simply look next door, at work, in the gym or at a bar. You may even be able to find a malicious meddling in-law or a long-lost creepy relative. Just take a good look around. There are plenty of people to pummel your good thing into a very bad deal. All you have to do is chill with them, buy 'em a beer, put them on speed dial and start spending all of your available free time with them.

Now, if you are single and want to ensure disaster in your life, one of the greatest ways to do so is to marry the wrong person. Guys, if you want chaos in your life, don't marry a woman of character, strength and virtue. Instead, just marry some chick because of her hair color, leg length and other physical features.

Make physicality the driving force that sends you to the altar. In addition, do not get to know her very well, and make the engagement super short. Don't listen to your parents' or friends' warnings about her. Make sure that she's not the same religion as you, that her mother's a busybody, that she is materialistic and has huge notions of entitlement, and that she has so many personalities they could form their own bowling team. Ditto for the girls.

The bottom line is this: When you feel the temptation to leave losers in the dust by switching jobs to get away from them, deleting their cell numbers from your phone or avoiding their calls and text messages altogether, you must realize that you are severing a powerful source for failure. So stop that immediately, or success may creep up on you. Yes, you might begin to gravitate toward the great—y'know, some positive, poisonous people who'll push you to excel.

If you're really serious about having a sad subsistence, it is important that you look for people who are decisively greedy, hateful, envious, contentious, deceptive, malicious gossips. Hunt for folks who are backstabbers, haters of good, insolent, proud and boastful. Don't worry, getting these people to be your friend will be easy—it's the loyal, dependable, virtuous people that are the ones who are tough to find.

Try to find those who are forever inventing new ways of messing up their lives while being disobedient to their parents and disrespectful to our nation. Find the miserable that treat their genitals like an amusement park, who lack understanding, who break their promises and who are heartless and unforgiving. They, my friend, are the ones who can help you (both directly and by osmosis) screw up your life in a beautiful and almost irretrievable way.

> *Health food may be good for the conscience,*
> *but Oreos taste a lot better.*
> ROBERT REDFORD

HABIT 5
BE A SELF-OBSESSED ME-MONKEY

Well, that's enough of me talking about me.
What do you think about me?
MARIAH CAREY

This is my fifth installment on how to significantly stall your life. I'm talkin' about bringing your thing to a grinding halt with rank ineffectiveness. This chapter's little ditty for the DDP is to engraft into your psyche the habit of being a self-obsessed me-monkey. If you're serious about living a life that will historically frame you out as a flop, then you must get this into your craw: Nobody and nothing matters but you and your little world.

Got it?

As a matter of fact—try saying that out loud and with passion.

Do it now.

C'mon, say it with me, "Nobody and nothing matters but me and my little world." Get it right: not God, not your spouse or kids, not your nation, not your state, not your city, not the godless, not the poor, not the infirm—it is just you and you alone that matters. Say it one more time, "Nobody and nothing matters but me and my little world."

There you go. Wasn't that b-e-e-YOU-tiful?

Did you feel the forces of darkness giving you a power surge? Pretty cool, eh? This new-found narcissistic motivation will take you right to the grave of being culturally ineffective, alone, unloved and without honor. Which is just what you, the DDP, are pursuing.

Uncut narcissism nukes the potential threat of greatness. True significance demands selfless sacrifice in the pursuit of the grand and noble. Because you have made a decisive leap away from importance, you must avoid sacrifices and selflessness like you would a ski parka in Iraq in the middle of August. Your job is to stay tuned to the petty minutiae that occupy that dipstick thing you call your life.

What is the difference between a catfish and a narcissist?
One's a bottom-crawling scum sucker, and the other's just a fish.
LIMLEY GILBERT

Let me give you an example of how to behave in a way that is in keeping with a narcissistic bent. Take me for example. I had quite a week, but I think I kept a pretty good distance from greatness. Here's how I handled my many challenges. Check it out:

- On Monday, one my maids messed up my African curio collection after I assiduously arranged them on the antique bookshelves that I bought from the Sultan of Obama-maumau. Just for that, I had her kneecaps shattered by Shawn Eckardt.

- On Tuesday, my butler ironed two pairs of my jeans wrong. You don't put a crease in jeans, Mr. French. Puh-leez. What about that do you not understand? For that, I had my gardener beat him with a small piece of garden hose.

- On Wednesday, Home Depot cheated me by not filling a can of Ralph Lauren metallic paint up to a full gallon. They put 126 ounces in the can instead of 128 ounces. I paid for a full gallon . . . a *gallon* . . . and I want a full gallon. I will never shop there again.

- On Thursday, my accountant didn't think the idea of me leasing a 645 Ci BMW was a wise move. I'm going to have him fired. But I think I'll wait until Christmas to do it. That'll teach him to deny me.

- On Friday, the French doors for my dog's doghouse did not come in as I was told. They are now going to be a week (a week!) late for installation. This is inexcusable. I plan on writing a six-page complaint letter to the president of the company.

- On Saturday, I found out that the giant altar I'm erecting to my writing and radio achievements will not fit in my aromatherapy room. I think I'm just going to have to sell the house.

- Finally, on Sunday, I went to church and heard a message that was a little too close to home, a little too long, not really my style, and too full of stuff that didn't directly appeal to me and my immediate requirements. So, I've decided to leave this church. Where will I go instead, you ask? Well, I have hired out a minister to come to my house every Sunday to minister to me and my pressing needs. I have even given this little gathering a name: The First Church of You'd Better Focus on Me or You'll be in My Dust.

It was a hectic 7 days, but after 12 hours at the spa, an affirmation session with my counselor and a mocha frappachino liberally laced with Xanax, I'm feeling back in good form. Now, if I can keep getting everyone to do what I say, this week should go smoothly as well. Anyway, using my example, you can see how to get wrapped around the axle regarding small things, turn that angst into anger, and then get even with everyone that wronged you until they learn that it is all about you.

> *I want you to want me. I need you to need me.*
> *I'd love you to love me. I'm beggin' you to beg me.*
> ROBIN ZANDER

If my initial exhortations, verbal confessions and own narcissistic example haven't helped you to be the auto-erotic, solipsistic yard ape you desire to be, please don't give up. I've got a few more items to toss into your court that will, along with the above advice, help you to grow in your delusions of grandeur and your need to be fawned over. If you stick with me, I guarantee that you will discover how to increase your utter disregard for the welfare of others.

Look, if you want high-grade, Hollywood/Washington, D.C.-type nasty narcissism, you must be focused. This is no game. This level of self-love is hard to achieve. You have to blow through common sense, your conscience, public opinion, the Holy Spirit, your grandmother calling you a jerk, and all kinds of other junk to become a truly biohazardous and egocentric person.

self-esteem: *n.* An erroneous appraisement.

AMBROSE BIERCE, *THE DEVIL'S DICTIONARY*

The following are six non-negotiables for the earnest egoist. If you hedge here, you can pretty much kiss your grab for gooey self-love goodbye. These must-haves were taken from Suite101.com and Sam Vaknin's Narcissistic Personality pages. (They have been paraphrased, abused, twisted and tortured by me for my own selfish needs.)

1. Get Crazy

You've got to get crazy with your fantasies of fame, power, unequalled brilliance, bodily beauty and sexual performance. Who cares if, in reality, you have a snowball's chance in hell for actually accomplishing your self-stroking pipe dreams? You shouldn't let the reality that you're a piece of luggage dissuade you from thinking that you can achieve omnipresent oneness.

2. Lie About Your Achievements

Do this compulsively and needlessly, and do it all the time about everything. Why do you need to do this? Lies will make you seem interesting and attractive, which could lead to another temporary job—or possibly a romantic fling with a very vapid person.

Yes, you should exaggerate everything you have done, and get to the point where you actually believe the stuff you spew. Being deeply self-deceived helps you to con others. Never forget that. You can practice your ruse while preparing your resume, when on dates, during initial business meetings or when you are recalling the days of your life with the unfortunate clods that have to listen to you speak.

To have nuclear-weapon-grade narcissism, you have to be your own reality stylist. Get creative.

3. Convince People You Know Everything

Demand to be recognized as an authority on everything, even though you don't know squat about anything you're talking about. Use your rich parents' names, some given title you occupy (but are woefully unqualified to hold) or other bombastic verbiage. Wave your doctorial bluster or holy poses in front of their faces. If all else fails, just flail your arms around to fool the easily dazzled into looking up to you. Who cares if you got what you have via sycophancy, nepotism or deceit?

If you're lacking props in having people receive you as an expert, you can go online to www.BogusGraduate Degrees.com and pick up a Masters degree. Or why not go ahead and get yourself a Doctorate? Who cares if you didn't earn your degree? What really matters are the prefixes you can now add to your name that will give you that added oomph to keep the credulous ogling you.

4. Believe in Your Heart that You Are Special

Get concretely convinced that you are unique. Also, tell yourself that because you are so special, only other unique and high-status individuals can understand you and, thus, you should only associate with these types of people. Y'know, it is hard being God's gift to the planet. One of the things that make it so hard for you is that there are so many plebeians out there that do not share your vain vision of enormity. *They* are the ones who keep you grounded and tethered to the planet. They must therefore be avoided at all costs.

> *Be constantly envious of other people's achievements*
> *and believe that they feel the same about you.*
> SAM VAKNIN

Besides, because these types of people don't have big names to drop, they keep your highness humbled, which is another great reason why you should steer clear of that crowd. You don't need people around you without true weightiness sensitivity, name recognition and nothing to immediately add to your future. What you need, what you must have and what you should crave is the affirmation and confirmation of the conferred. Yes, you've got to require excessive admiration, adulation, attention and affirmation if you truly want to be a self-obsessed, sick little me-monkey.

5. Advertise the Fact that You Are Unstable

Do everything possible to make people fear you, and try to become notorious for having temper tantrums. Go frickin' nuts if you don't get your way. Have people bow in terror of your persona and needs. This works wonders on wafty people who are easily controlled.

One thing that'll assist you in drumming up demonic rage is to increase your notions of entitlement. Yes, an expectation of unreasonable, special and favorable priority treatment will set the stage for crazy fits of fury when someone drops the ball around you.

Having ridiculous notions of how important you are will help you get past the weird feelings you have about being overly demanding, dramatic and wrathfully exacting. Anger is an awesome little ditty in helping you to be

Why should we only honor
those that die
upon the field of battle?
A man may show
as reckless a courage
in entering into the abyss
of himself.

WILLIAM BUTLER YEATS

DON'T FALL
FOR THIS
NONSENSE!

interpersonally exploitative (helping you to use others to achieve your goals). Yes, merge your haughty behaviors with rage when you are frustrated, contradicted or confronted and watch the good times roll as you achieve your goals by acting like a toad.

Oh, and I almost forgot this piece of sweet wisdom: Along with your narcissistic wrath, you need to learn how to suddenly shift emotionally when you are dealing with people. Don't just stay angry all the time—that could lose people. What you must master is the ability to flip-flop between sadism and altruism, abuse and "love," ignoring and caring, abandoning and clinging, and viciousness and remorse. These insane mood swings will spawn a walking-on-eggshells mentality in your friends that will help you get what you want out of them.

6. Don't Be True-Blue

Undervalue the people and places that have added to your life. Yes, heartlessly and off-handedly abandon those who have helped you. Dispose of people, places, partnerships and friendships without a second thought. After all, they didn't help you get where you are—I mean, not really. Sure, they put up with your monotonous monologues and seemingly unending conversations about your day, supported you through many difficult times and gave you money to get by on when you were forced to sell your blood for some quick cash, but other than that, they weren't that great of a support base.

7. Avoid Christians, the Bible and Church

Here's a final warning for those who are determined to be self-obsessed me-monkeys: Stay away from the teachings of Jesus Christ. The Word of God will absolutely ruin your selfishness. It will mess with your time, your talent and your treasure. It will require you to speak out and act selflessly when it is inconvenient for you. It will put the onus on you to love people you don't want to mess with, care for people you couldn't care less about, give portions of your income to those who are in need, and forgive people you'd rather crush. What kind of smack is that?

That's for people who are grand, and you, my friend, are not grand. Since you don't seek to be anywhere near that which is noble, I would run from Christ's teachings like Newt Gingrich would from Janet Reno if she tried to kiss him while wearing a pleather cat suit.

> *The last time I saw him, he was walking down*
> *Lover's Lane holding his own hand.*
> BILLY "HOUND DOG" BILLARITO

HABIT 6
LEARN TO KISS UP

kiss up: *v.* To behave obsequiously; to fawn over someone; to please someone in order to gain a personal advantage. Synonyms: bootlicking, fawning, sycophantic, toadyish.

Herewith is the sixth key to crippling your existence: Learn to kiss up to people. Historically, effective people, who have shaped society for the better, have been people of conviction. Since you've determined to be a highly ineffective dupe, you must avoid standing for truth the same way Gandhi shunned food. Yes, conviction, taking your stance for time-tested verities, has been known to cause nations to change and people to prosper—and since your goal is to be a troll, feckless compliance is a foundational key to unlock mediocrity's door.

This capitulating spirit will not only make you a craven hush-mouth but will also simultaneously assist secularists in hijacking our country though simple lack of protest. Yes, by your saying and being nothing and trembling in the face of public opinion, you—the supposed traditional-value-honoring American—will help hamstring our Stars and Stripes.

Let me roll this thing out for you.

For the last 40 years, there has been a belligerent, systematic secularization of the United States by the liberal thought police. These individuals have sought to remove from all public sectors of society any semblance of biblical values, all influence of religious institutions and all sacred symbolism.

These anti-religious relativists reject the notion of an absolute standard of truth that is applicable to all people, in all places and at all times. For this cabal, there is no transcendent norm of right or wrong, only pleasure and pain. For them, because God does not exist or at least cannot be solidly defined, well, then, nothing is prohibited.

Yes, for these "thinkers," everything is endlessly open to question and to change. Everything is permitted. Nothing is banned and literally nothing is bizarre. The secularists envision a modern America with a moral climate similar to Sodom right before God lit it up.

There's nothing wrong with Southern California that
a rise in the ocean level wouldn't cure.
ROSS MACDONALD

Check it out: Feeding feverishly off postmodernism's compost heap of historical amnesia, secularists reject an objective standard of truth. Thus, in their would-be world, authorities are leveled, records are rewritten, the autonomous self becomes the sole judge of reality, cultures are equalized, style reigns over substance, power is deified, and the "victims" run the circus and are conveniently licensed to lie.

In the PoMo world where truth is dead, power becomes the operative principle of speech. The results are conformity and bullying—you know, the stuff you see on ABC, CBS, NBC, CNN, Bravo, VH1 and MTV on a daily basis as they pulverize the religious traditionalist with every banal broadcast. The effect is that the secular revolutionaries have created a rock-solid environment of political correctness—and God help you if you rustle their feathers by not parroting their opinions.

The person who champions a traditional view of truth and not hype, stands for the historical record and not the hysterical read, and believes that biblically based, previously proven, transcendent standards should continue to serve as an external pattern to govern our nation's character will endure more scorn than Britney Spears on her last reality show.

A great person who loves God and the way this nation was originally constituted will stand up against this hijacking of our nation by the secularists. Yes, the grand and the noble will not lie down and roll up in the fetal position when God's truth isn't en vogue. Great people side with truth even when it's detested.

The bold that hold an objective biblical view of right and wrong will stand up in this age when evil has been twisted into appearing good and good has been twisted into appearing evil. They will do this no matter what the cost and no matter how hard they'll be slammed in the media, in liberal chat rooms or on liberal blogs. The great will not neglect the truth, contradict the truth or be careless with the truth. They understand that if they do so, they will, as Os Guinness says, have "stumbled into a carelessness that [they] can ill afford."

This is the spirit, which you, the gutless nutless wonder, must avoid at all costs. Because you desire above all else to be a DDP, your concerns should not run toward upholding truth in a day of lies, hype and spin. That would toss you into the substantial bullpen. Rather, you must blow off the verities of holy writ and its time-tested values in favor of that which is popular.

If you want to get to the top, prepare to kiss a lot of the bottom.

DESPAIR.COM

Now, I must warn you that as you set out to embrace the chameleon's life of political correctness, being a spineless and ardent yes-man will initially bring you favor and, therefore, some measure of success. But don't fear.

Your success will be limited and short lived, and you will quickly be forgotten. So don't sweat it if in your pursuit of ignominy you observe some personal growth. It will only be a temporary success at best that will not strangle your long-term desires for dearth.

Okay, so now that you've decided that your interest is in being liked rather than being effective, let's get busy in developing your doormat personality. To skirt the victory that comes with being bold in your beliefs, there are a couple of things that you must put between your cheek and gum and chew.

First off, you must deeply believe that nothing is worth fighting for, much less dying for. Work this mantra into your mind: "Peace is always preferable to conflict—even if the times demand an ideological or physical throw down." Lock your soul's sights on being a survivor, not a warrior. Never mind that surviving is sometimes the worst thing that can happen to you when the situation calls for you to do something sacrificial that might cost you a party invitation or a pound of flesh.

Segueing off the survival-at-all-costs motif, the capitulator must quickly learn to become an excellent kisser of the *gluteus maximus*. You've got to get good at this if you want to shed from your soul every ounce of dignity.

Self-respect, honor, forthrightness and the determination to stand alone and oppose that which is wrong will hurt your desires for a defective life. If this stuff somehow becomes part of your MO . . . well . . . you're doomed, as eventually it will enable you to become something. And we don't want that to happen, do we?

In order to succeed at acquiring a bland existence, you must remember that getting along is more important than what's right or wrong—no matter who or what you have to sell out. Your focus should be on being cautious about preserving your reputation and social standing, not standing up for righteousness and truth.

Therefore, rid from your makeup any thought that might make you dangerous to the current cultural and political constructs that keep people domesticated tools of the machine. What you want to do is expunge from existence that wild hair that keeps you from bowing to the powers that be, forbids you from buying what everyone is selling and keeps you from embracing those ideologies that you know are utter bunk. Corral your common sense and conviction to the place where you're easily owned, manipulated, bowed, dazzled, domesticated, repressed and ashamed. In other words, make the opinions of others your god.

Its name is Public Opinion. It is held in reverence.
It settles everything. Some think it is the voice of God.
Loyalty to petrified opinion never yet broke
a chain or freed a human soul.

MARK TWAIN

Finally, to become proficient at puckering up to others, stand in front of the mirror and pretend that someone just told you something completely ridiculous. Or that you just saw something that is atrocious—either politically, culturally or ecclesiastically. Now, instead of actually saying or doing anything about the situation, simply bow and say, "Wow, that makes a lot of sense. I completely agree with everything I've just heard."

In addition, you may want to roll over and pee in your pants. Definitely do not stand up, speak up, rile up, throw up or toss empty takeout food containers at the TV. Don't even roll your eyes or do anything that would remotely suggest that you think whatever you saw or heard is complete and utter horse dooky. You can and *must* erase from your psyche every ounce of common sense and courage to get to that coveted place of being a blank and soulless slate.

To expedite this ickyness, I'll leave you with a simple exercise that you can do in the privacy of your own home.

All you need is a mirror and a few minutes. Here we go now. First, wet your whistle, and now pucker. Release. Pucker. Release. Do this for eight minutes, seven times a day for the next six months, and I guarantee you'll be well on your way to nowhere. Drop what you're doing right now and pucker. Release. Pucker. Release. There you go. That was easy enough, eh?

Now, run outside without any sense of belief, firmly convinced that there is no right or wrong, and be the convictionless, glute-kissing aficionado we all know you can be. For certain, this wet-noodle-like spine you've embraced will keep you within the complicit herd and not at the head of the pack where success and change are found.

Physical courage,
which despises all danger,
will make a man brave
in one way;
and moral courage,
which despises all opinion,
will make a man brave
in another.

CHARLES CALEB COTTON

DON'T FALL FOR THIS NONSENSE!

If, after reading all of the information above, you're still having a hard time shutting your mouth when faced with the ridiculous in our culture, there is one last drastic measure you might want to consider: Go and have your spine removed. It's hard to stand up against injustice (or anything else for that matter) when you can't even pick yourself up off the floor. Lack of a proper endoskeleton has been known to greatly reduce people's effectiveness in maintaining that protesting spirit.

Think about all the spineless wimps you have met in your life. Were any of them spirited motivators who were able to stand up for their beliefs and enact real change in the world? Certainly not. Like jellyfish in the sea, they just floated wherever the waves happened to take them until they washed up on shore and dried out in the sun. And that, my friend, is a beautiful picture of what your life can also become.

Having a backbone will mess up things in your quest for loser greatness. It will make you want to stand up and intellectually and physically fight, if need be, against all the crud that is out there in our society. It will make you want to *believe* in something. These traits are the marks of the consequential, and because you are determined to be a decidedly defective

person, you may want to go ahead and schedule that
doctor's appointment.

> *I require three things of a man.*
> *He must be handsome, ruthless and stupid.*
> DOROTHY PARKER

HABIT 7

BECOME A FEAR-ADDLED, BACKWARD-LOOKING HAMSTER

Until you have the courage to lose sight of the shore, you will not know the terror of being forever lost at sea.

DESPAIR.COM

Being a bold risk taker will make you tough, and if you don't shed this yahoo, Git-R-Done spirit, sooner or later you're going to succeed at something. Seeing as how you've set your sights on being an emotional limp noodle, you want to avoid boldness like Tom Cruise avoids Brooke Shields and Matt Lauer.

What you've got to do is adopt a motto that will keep your soul anchored to angst. Yes, you need a life-defining phrase that you can refer to whenever you are tempted to be adventurous and dicey. Mottos are powerful. Consider Nike's motto: *Just Do It.* Supposedly, people who buy Nike products want to actually "do" stuff and not just talk about it.

The other day when I was surfing the Internet for valuable 411 to help you destroy your life, I stumbled across one particular church's website that caught my attention. It's a church in South Florida that is pastored by this really arrogant, over-moussed twit who thinks he's funny and smart (what a clod). Anyway, they have a maxim: "Clash Church: Bold. Wild. Free." All I've got to say is . . . Whatever.

You ought to go to their website at ClashChurch.Com and check out these idiots. But don't linger too long on their website or their message, music and videos will start pumping adrenaline into your flagging and floppy back-side. And that, as I've repeatedly warned you throughout this book, could cause you to actually get a life.

Back to having a motto . . . you want a motto, creed, dogma, axiom, proverb, truism, cliché, platitude, tired expression or insipid and thoughtless "go to" slogan that you can live and fail by. I'm talkin' about something you can put on your desk, shove into your brain and spit out of your mouth that will from here on out frame you for substantial failure versus audacious accomplishment.

For instance, what about something like . . .

- *Don't* do it.
- Splat happens.
- Why bother?
- I don't have enough money.
- I could die.
- I could go broke.
- I could get hurt.
- I could look dumb.
- I love my ruts.
- I have no guts!
- I love comfort.
- Don't challenge me.

- Tread on me.
- I'm the devil's doormat.
- Embrace fear!
- Know who to blame.
- Whine and dine.
- Hope is overrated.

Having your crosshairs buried on the bulls-eye of living a life of fear, you've got to expunge from your constituent makeup any form of risk taking. So, herewith are seven principles that will slay any residual faith or boldness that may lie within you and help you to gnaw your fingernails in fear like a schizophrenic ferret.

Do not step up the stairs. Content yourself with staring up the steps.
SWIMMY MORPQAAD

1. Think Too Much Before Taking a Risk
If you ever determine that you'd like to go for something that's right and worthy (which you shouldn't), you must immediately begin to think too much in order to keep yourself from actually doing what you're contemplating.

In relation to that dream that's rattling around in that whirring tin brain of yours, you must think about how much money it will cost, how others have tried and failed, how you're woefully unsuited to handle the task, and whether or not you have the right look or the right connections to accomplish your goal. Why must you do this? Well, junior, it is because hesitating will psyche you out. Yes, over-analyzing the situation will cause you to balk instead of walk. Say this with me: "Think and shrink. Think and shrink. Think and shrink."

Thinking too much is also a good way to mask your fear. You don't want people to view you as a nervous and spineless newt—even though, if you followed my advice in the last chapter, you undoubtedly are. Nor do you want others to see you as a sniveling, cringing, backward-gazing goof. Therefore, you need to mask your fear behind supposed contemplation and analysis.

To really pull off this farcical charade, make sure you have the appropriate costume and props to hide your dread. For instance, when your friends come over to hang out with you, there is a probability that they may ask you about your goals in life. Because you don't want them to discover that you are growing more chicken by the minute, do the following:

- Wear glasses. They make you look thoughtful.
- Grow a goatee. This will make you look radical and scary, like Anton LaVey or something.
- Wear a corduroy jacket with elbow patches on top of a white A&F oxford shirt—untucked, of course. This is shabby chic. It says you care but don't care.
- Smoke a pipe, or clove cigarettes.
- Scrunch your forehead a lot. People view this as if you're in deep thought . . . trying to figure out something.
- Hold your hand to your mouth and say, "Hmm . . ."
- Have classical music playing in the background.
- Have CSPAN on the tube (with the volume down) and all your computers in the house on websites that correspond to your supposed goal in life.
- Distribute various fancy books and newspapers throughout your apartment. Leave them opened like you've just been reading through them, again. Moreover, print a lot of corresponding graphs and pie charts. Yeah, that's it . . . pie charts. Lots of pie charts! Get some colored ones. It'll slay 'em. They'll think you're wisely on fire with your desire. This is gold, baby, pure gold.

This subterfuge and "thoughtful" posturing will easily lull your duller friends into assuming that you have goals but are taking your time about working toward them and are simply being shrewd. They will never guess the reality that you're just a gutless wonder who is, essentially, afraid to jump in.

2. If You Jump, Jump Small

Should you for some reason not take my advice and end up going for something in life, to keep your chances high for being a slug, you'll need to hold back when you do jump into whatever you're jumping into.

Yep, going for it, with reserve, is also an effective veil behind which you can easily hide your fearful, vapid soul. How come? Well, think about it. People see you going for it and doing "the do." But in your heart, you know that you ain't gonna do what you're prattling on about—because mediocrity is your god.

Therefore, do not *under any circumstance* fully commit yourself to any endeavor, be it vocationally, relationally or spiritually. Yes, hold back and always have a way out . . . an escape route that you can take should things get rough and require too much from you.

One constant mantra the mediocre mumble under their baby breath is this: "Well, if this doesn't work, I'll always have [insert something lame] to fall back on." With this type of halfhearted commitment careening around that chicken heart of yours, I guarantee that even if you have a lapse of judgment and do get ambitious, your reservations will efficiently and eventually murder your forward momentum in a positive direction. Which is nice.

> *The road to hell is paved with works in progress.*
> PHILIP ROTH

3. Let Failure Suck the Living Daylights Out of You

Successful people have this tawdry slop of allowing failure to teach them lessons. They think of failure as an opportunity to learn and grow wiser. This is uncut, china-white bunk that you should flee from if—that is, *if*—you want to truly lose in life, mi amigo. To become the frozen deer in the headlights, don't ever try to figure out why you failed or were rejected in a particular situation and try to milk some sage lesson from the dilemma. No, you should just sit on your duff and give up. Forever.

4. Cower in the Covers

When you encounter failure, do not under any circumstance get up and get moving in the morning. Stay in bed and have a panic attack. If you get up and get moving, it is highly likely that energy, faith and hope might hit you via a friend, a song or an inspirational story on TV or the radio. Therefore, stay in bed and freak. Let your imagination run amok in conjuring up various things that are going to get you.

5. Sing Depressing Songs

Pick your favorite depressing tune and sing your butt off until gloom drips from your soul like insincerity from Ryan Seacrest. Depressing and negative songs are a great source of melancholy, which is a climactic condition that you should covet.

> *Yesterday I got so old I felt like I could die.*
> THE CURE, "INBETWEEN DAYS"

6. For God's Sake, Don't Exercise

Exercise gives you attitude, and you want to avoid attitude because that can lead to altitude. So stay inside. Breathe stale air. Let your muscles atrophy. Allow lethargy to zap the oomph and chutzpah that come with regular work-outs. Exercise will transfer to you 24/7 and make you feel better about yourself—and you don't want that.

7. Repeat Negative Scenarios Over and Over in Your Head
Rehearse in your noggin how people have married the wrong person, gone bankrupt, had car wrecks, died in attacks by stingrays, gotten sick going to a public bathroom, suffocated in Saran Wrap, developed cancer from using their cell phones, had a pet attack them, had friends betray them, or have lost money in the stock market. Then tell yourself how all of this could happen to *you*.

> *Wow, you guys, Disneyworld really is fun. It must be*
> *fun to work here . . . although the biggest drawback to*
> *working in a theme park is that you must live in con-*
> *stant fear of deadly terrorist attacks.*
> DEBBIE DOWNER

Essentially, make a list of every bad thing that's ever happened to you or anyone else, whether living or dead, and tell yourself this will probably also happen to you.

One secret that will help you keep the negative info fresh and effective is to talk to yourself in different accents.

My favorite and most useful voices are a high-pitched, sort-of-Chinese accent; a thick, drunken Scottish brogue; and my imitation of a screaming, middle-aged, female Isadshi-Koseshi warrior. E-mail me and tell me which burr worked the best for you. You can reach me at mail@youcan'tbe serious.com.

If fear is cultivated
it will become stronger.
If faith is cultivated
it will achieve mastery.
We have a right to believe
that faith is the stronger emotion
because it is positive
whereas fear is negative.
JOHN PAUL JONES

DON'T FALL FOR **THIS** **NONSENSE!**

Are you a Christian? To help fear foul your soul's spark plugs, remove from your mind and heart any thought that God will protect you, empower you or provide for you. Convince yourself that He won't give you wisdom or bless you with more than you could ever ask for or imagine. Tell yourself that you are so far gone that God couldn't possibly forgive, redeem or restore you after you blow it—that this stuff is reserved for God's favorites . . . y'know, the ones on Christian TV . . . and not you. To truly become despondent, you need to abandon any hope that heaven will come to your aid.

In conclusion, if you're feeling like you do not have enough paralyzing fears, herewith is a list of various phobias and the famous people, animals and nations that have them. These are designer fears, some of which are very rare, that many well-known, pretty people are satiated with. Just think of how you will not only be sidelined with dread but also in the company of famous phobaholics!

A

Ablutophobia—Fear of washing or bathing (the French)

Agateophobia—Fear of insanity (Bill O'Reilly)

Anglophobia—Fear of English culture (Osama Bin Laden)

Anuptaphobia—Fear of staying single (a bunch of 30- and 40-year-olds I know)

Apeirophobia—Fear of infinity (Honda)

Arsonphobia—Fear of fire (firecrackers)

Ataxophobia—Fear of disorder or untidiness (Martha Stewart)

Atelophobia—Fear of imperfection (Martha Stewart)

Automysophobia—Fear of being dirty (Martha Stewart)

B

Bibliophobia—Fear of books (50 Cent)

Batrachophobia—Fear of amphibians (Pharaoh)

C

Cacophobia—Fear of ugliness (Paris Hilton)

Caligynephobia—Fear of beautiful women (George Castanza)

Chorophobia—Fear of dancing (me)

Coprastasophobia—Fear of constipation (me)

D

Decidophobia—Fear of making decisions (John Kerry)

Didaskaleinophobia—Fear of going to school (Pink Floyd)

Dikephobia—Fear of justice (Tony Soprano)

Doraphobia—Fear of fur or skins of animals (PETA)

Dutchphobia—Fear of the Dutch (Nigel Powers)

E

Ecclesiophobia—Fear of church (Marilyn Manson)

Eleutherophobia—Fear of freedom (China)

Elurophobia—Fear of cats (Mickey Mouse)

Euphobia—Fear of hearing good news (CBS, NBC, ABC and CNN)

F

Francophobia—Fear of French Culture (Larry the Cable Guy)

Frigophobia—Fear of cold (Southern Californians)

G

Gamophobia—Fear of marriage (most men)

Gerascophobia—Fear of growing old (The Who)

Gymnophobia—Fear of nudity (Al Sharpton)

H

Hedonophobia—Fear of feeling pleasure (Church folks)

Helminthophobia—Fear of being infested with worms (Herod)

Hexakosioihexekontahexaphobia—Fear of the number 666 (*Left Behind* readers)

Hippopotomonstrosesquippedaliophobia—Fear of long words (Lil' Kim)

Hoplophobia—Fear of firearms (the deer that I'm hunting)

I

Ichthyophobia—Fear of fish (worms)

Iophobia—Fear of poison (Socrates)

J

Japanophobia—Fear of the Japanese (tarpon)

K

Kainolophobia—Fear of anything new (Antiques Road-
show)

Kakorrhaphiophobia—Fear of defeat (New York Yankees)

L

Levophobia—Fear of things to the left side of the body
(Rush Limbaugh)

Ligyrophobia—Fear of loud noises (Yosemite Sam)

Lutraphobia—Fear of otters (the fish that otters eat, I
guess)

Lyssophobia—Fear of rabies or of becoming mad (Tom
Cruise)

M

Macrophobia—Fear of long waits (Joe Pesci)

Menophobia—Fear of menstruation (all married men)

Metallophobia—Fear of metal (Michael Bolton)

Microbiophobia—Fear of microbes (Howard Hughes)

Microphobia—Fear of small things (Shaq)

Motorphobia—Fear of automobiles (Lindsay Lohan)

Musophobia or Muriphobia—Fear of mice (elephants)

Mythophobia—Fear of myths, stories or false statements
(Dan Rather)

N

Nosocomephobia—Fear of hospitals (Evil Knieval)

Novercaphobia—Fear of step-mothers (step-children)

Nucleomituphobia—Fear of nuclear weapons (the Earth)

Numerophobia—Fear of numbers (English majors)

O

Obesophobia—Fear of gaining weight (the Olsen twins)

Ophthalmophobia—Fear of being stared at (Gwyneth Paltrow)

Optophobia—Fear of opening one's eyes (anyone who's ever slept with their contact lenses still in)

Ouranophobia—Fear of heaven (atheists)

P

Papaphobia—Fear of the Pope (Sinead O'Connor)

Paralipophobia—Fear of neglecting duty or responsibility (decidedly undefective people)

Paraphobia—Fear of sexual perversion (the Church Lady)

Pedophobia—Fear of children (those who didn't take the time to raise theirs properly)

Peladophobia—Fear of bald people (supermodels)

Peniaphobia—Fear of poverty (Donald Trump)

Phengophobia—Fear of daylight or sunshine (LeStadt)

Phronemophobia—Fear of thinking (un . . . uh . . .)
Pogonophobia—Fear of bearding (Italian women)

R
Ranidaphobia—Fear of frogs (Egyptians)
Rhytiphobia—Fear of getting wrinkles (Joan Rivers)
Russophobia—Fear of Russians (anyone who has married a Russian woman)

S
Satanophobia—Fear of Satan (Linda Blair and Emily Rose)
Scolionophobia—Fear of school (me)
Selachophobia—Fear of sharks (everyone who saw Jaws)
Sesquipedalophobia—Fear of long words (Mike Tyson)
Sinistrophobia—Fear of things to the left (Sean Hannity)
Sociophobia—Fear of society or people in general (Ted Kazinsky)

T
Tachophobia—Fear of speed (manatees)
Taphephobia—Fear of being buried alive (that would be me again)
Taurophobia—Fear of bulls (dead bullfighters)
Theologicophobia—Fear of theology (agnostics)

Thermophobia—Fear of heat (Al Gore)

Toxiphobia—Fear of poison (Rasputin)

Tyrannophobia—Fear of tyrants (freed Iraqis)

U

Uranophobia—Fear of heaven (Hugh Hefner)

Urophobia—Fear of urine or urinating (people with bladder infections)

V

Vestiphobia—Fear of clothing (nudists)

W

Wiccaphobia—Fear of witches and witchcraft (anyone who saw *The Blair Witch Project*)

X

Xenophobia—Fear of strangers (Camus)

Xerophobia—Fear of dryness (Jergens)

Xyrophobia—Fear of razors (Nick Nolte)

Try everything once except incest and folk dancing.
SIR THOMAS BEECHAM

HABIT **8**

QUIT WHEN THE GOING GETS TOUGH

Don't allow your conscience the right to approve of your conduct;
that could cause you to turn and go in a noble direction when
what you should really do is quit.

WOUNDED MOOSE

The eighth habit of the hapless is to consistently quit when the going gets tough. Yeah, the amazing messes of humanity are uniform in their weak resolve to stick it out when stuff really starts to hit the fan. Difficulties erode the DDP's doggedness to do the nominal things that most normal people do to live. This is good, goodly and goodish.

There are several ways to work a wussy spirit to warp your life, and I'm here to help make sure you have a miserable day, week, month and year. Are you ready? I said, ARE YOU READY? Yell now, out loud, no matter where you are or whom you are with, "I am ready to quit when the going gets tough! I am a mouse! I want to be—no, I *will* be—weak, insipid, characterless and tame! I am wussy; hear me roar! I AM . . . *WUSSMAN!* (or *WUSS-WOMAN!*)"

That felt groovy, didn't it?

Shouting, declaring and proclaiming your lack of readiness for change internally sets the stage for a militant manifestation of the external malformations of the crummy life that you now seek. But in addition to just yelling out loud, there are four additional steps that you must also take. These four things will help you to make mountains out of molehills and cause you to melt like a little Ghirardelli girlie man when you're mildly opposed.

Let's do this.

1. Lack Purpose

Don't have a clear-cut purpose backed up by commitment to see things through. Lack of clarity helps to dramatically reduce any risk of success. You should, therefore, keep aimlessly careening around the planet. Should you not be an aimless wanderer with weak resolve and currently have the corrupting influence of focus and commitment still trying to attach itself to you, you can lose these vices by becoming distracted and preferring comfort over duty.

Here's whatcha gotta do.

To lose focus (which brings commitment, which equates to prosperity), you should get caught up in peripheral purposeless tasks that take time away from the central mondo themes in which you might be currently involved. It doesn't really matter what you get into as long as it keeps you distracted from the stuff that really matters in life.

Say, for instance, you want your marriage to collapse and your kids' lives to be ruined. If this is what you seek, you need to obsess about work, hang out with your dillweed buddies a bunch, spend all of your free time occupied with some hobby or sport, have an affair with that crazy hostess chick at Chili's, or do something else that doesn't directly involve your family.

The detachment you will develop from your important family via these asinine activities will provide you with a weak will when you begin to bump up against the various trials in marriage and childrearing. The lack of concentration or sense of obligation that will be crafted through tangential pursuits will suck the life out of any spirit to war for that which is worthy and weighty. That advice alone, my friend, is worth the price of this book. You owe me a beer.

2. Lack Drive and Energy

Sporadically and non-energetically work at what you're after. This one is a beauty. Calvin Coolidge said, "Persistence and a determination to succeed are prerequisites for success." Notice that Mr. Coolidge did not say talent, brains or ability, but *persistence*. When people work off and on at something, it demonstrates that they are just tinkerers and not tenacious about what they blather on and on about.

As a DDP, you must beware of pursuing something relentlessly, alone and unapplauded, because this smack will land you in the sweet spot of life. No, if you want to be a quality quitter, you must show intermittent interest and an irregular investment of energy.

Think about it.

Irregular attention to something doesn't marry you to a particular person, project or cause. Thus, when difficulties arise—which they will, because you're not down-the-funnel committed to these people and duties—you can quit with little opposition. Can you dig it? I knew you could. Quitting is a piece of cake when you're a non-zealous dabbler in whatever you put your hand to. Say with me now, "I can be half-hearted!"

3. Be Easily Influenced to Despair

Be open to negative and discouraging influences from foes, friends, family members, books, *MAD* magazine articles and local news reports. Those who accomplish great things are fairly firm in their resolve to not hang around negative people. Successful people understand the force that some foul negative weed can have on their dreams. Therefore, they avoid discouraging people like Donald Trump avoids soul kissing Rosie. Your goal is to be a troll, and in order to accomplish your end of ickyness, you've got to be a quitter. And to be a quitter, it is imperative that you have a lot of folks around you who are encouraging you to give up.

Yes, to be an accomplished loser, you're going to need some assistance in the form of harsh criticism and gloominess. Most people need not look any further than their family or friends.

What's beautiful about looking to your family for this is that they already know you. They've seen you grow up. They've seen you wet your bed, pick your nose and cry during *Oprah*. They know all your weak points, foibles and why you shouldn't and couldn't ever accomplish anything that might shame their lackluster life. They are a great source of despair whenever you're tempted with a worthy pursuit that may leave them languishing back in Wussville, choking on your dust.

Therefore, readily share your dreams with your negative Darwinian holdover next of kin. They will joyfully tell you that you're too stupid, too old, too young, too poor, too uneducated or too whatever it takes to suck the wind right out of your sails.

You must never, under any circumstance, leave your negative family members if you want to lead a decidedly defective life. Never. You got it? Dismal, grim carnage and doom-saying relatives are a must-have for a life of hell on

Earth. Do not, I say, *do not* move away from them or refuse to receive their calls. If you're determined to quit when the going gets tough, you'll need their negative support when you feel tempted to stay the course.

4. Make Up Lots of Excuses

Use excuses and alibis to explain why you haven't accomplished anything. For instance, when my editors told me that this book is not only vapid but running short on the contracted word count, I told them that the reason it was weak and incomplete was because I was rejected in the womb and because I suffer from low blood sugar, which makes me unable to think or write for long periods of time.

Also, the medical marijuana I smoke has really been killing my productivity levels, but if I don't smoke it, I have panic attacks, which eventually lead to trips to the ER— and that *really* eats up the clock.

What was I talking about?

Oh yeah, excuses and alibis for why people cannot get their act together. Essentially, what I would do is just blame the government. Those in office probably hate you and are thus keeping you from being productive.

Using excuses, being open to negativity, taking sporadic and non-energetic actions, and allowing your focus to get fractured are brilliant cripplers of one's resolve to stick things out. As you massage these four foundational foul funky factoids into your psyche, you will quickly and increasingly find that weakness is becoming part of your personality.

Weakness is good. Good for losing. Good for prepping one for disaster, debt and discontentment. Good for getting you to the point where all you want to do in life is just give up. For the DDP, reaching that place is sweet indeed.

HABIT 9

RIP PEOPLE OFF

*I think they ought to just go ahead and legalize
stealing . . . actually, there is something
funny about getting away with it.*

MIKE JUDGE

Rip People Off

Habit 10

DELIVER LESS THAN PROMISED

*Mediocrity takes a lot less time, and most people
won't notice the difference until it's too late.*

The tenth habit of decidedly defective people is to deliver less than promised. Let me give you an example of what I'm talking about. I don't know if you noticed or not, but you paid $13 for 10 habits, and there was nothing in chapter 9. That's what you do. Hype it and then rip 'em off. Deliver less than promised.

Perhaps Abraham Lincoln summed it up best when he said:

> Any people anywhere, being inclined and having the power, have the right to rise up, and shake off the existing government, and form a new one that suits them better. This is a most valuable—a most sacred right—a right, which we hope and believe, is to liberate the world.

See how easy it is? That quote had absolutely nothing to do with anything that I am talking about. I just Googled "Lincoln quotes" and took the first one I found that filled up a few lines. Once you get the hang of it, you'll find that ripping off people is a lot easier than it sounds.

Within your circle of friends and family, raise expectations by promising to do things with them and then back out at the last minute because "something important came up." Within no time, you will find that people no longer trust you or depend on you, which is great because they will no longer expect anything from you. As an added bonus, they will no longer want to be around you, which will further enable you to live out your DDP dreams.

If you're a businessman, you must plug the heck out of whatever goods, services or merchandise you're selling so that consumers will spend their hard-earned money for your junk. Of course, your deep dishonesty in business, although it might initially bring you prosperity, will not be long lasting. People will eventually catch on to you and drop you like Queen Elizabeth would a pickled pig's foot.

Another excellent way to deliver less than what you have promised is to simply . . .

AN ADDENDUM FOR THE
DDP DUM-DUM:
SIN AND SIN AGAIN

Hey buddy. You've just finished *10 Habits of Decidedly Defective People*. Pretty cool, eh? Normally I would not congratulate you for accomplishing anything, but in this case you have accomplished that which will assist in your collapse. And as Borat would say, that is "very nice."

I bet you feel excited and probably a little overwhelmed. Kind of shell-shocked with both the wealth of information I've just offloaded onto you and the dizzying dilemma of where to begin. In addition to those ditties, there probably is some nagging doubt as to whether or not the defective life can truly be yours.

First of all, you must simmer down now. I said simmer down now. Chill. Relax. Quit stressing out about not achieving your disastrous desires.

Second, you must trust me and believe with all your heart that you can be a DDP if you will simply obey the 10 habits I have outlined in this book. Doubt and unbelief regarding whether or not you'll succeed at a disastrous life cannot be tolerated, as these two negative forces will destroy any hope you have for a desperate existence.

I know, I sound like a broken record. I said, I know, I sound like a broken record, record, record, record, record, record, record, but hear me loud and clear: You must have faith that you too can be hopeless. B-E-L-I-E-V-E that you can put the funk in dysfunction.

Being a DDP, you're probably not used to getting so much information or accustomed to implementing any type of plan. I know how you feel, dude. Reading more than 100 pages can be a real pain in the butt, and adhering to 10 habits can also be hemorrhoidal.

So, in an attempt to help you fulfill your dreary dreams and move past the paralysis that can come with doubt, let me give you seven easy sins to secure your place in the pits. These are simple and primal abominations that a squirrel that has been eating paint chips and chasing them down with toxic sludge could do. As a matter of fact, you will probably be able to turn your life into a train wreck with just these seven vices, which means you just wasted your time with all that 10 habits stuff I wrote. Good for you. Wasting time, as you now know, is a prerequisite for privation and pain.

For the *coup de grace,* herewith are seven transgressions that will ruin you both here and in eternity. A double whammy . . . a two-fer. Pretty awesome, eh? Follow the dictates of these damnable ditties and you'll attract

God's disdain, which always helps when you are hell-bent for leather.

Let's do this.

Are you ready to embrace sin like never before? I know you are. And because you loathe that which is holy, just and good, I present you with Satan's select: the seven deadly sins. "Deadly." What a cool word. Say it with me: "deadly." Did you get goose bumps? I did. Dead dreams, hopes, relationships, careers and even your very soul can be lost with these bad boys. So let me get busy and show you, the DDP, how to bring your thing down to hellish ruin.

1. Pride

Pride, as Os Guinness states, "Historically [has been] seen as the first, worst, and most prevalent of the seven deadly sins. It is either the source or the chief component of all other sin. Pride is also the first of the sins of the spirit, which are 'cold' but highly respectable. Its source is neither the world nor the flesh, but the devil. This first vice is unique in that it is the one vice of which its perpetrator is frequently unaware."*

---

* By the way, you should shun reading Os Guinness. He's one of those Christian hope freaks. Whatever. Another by the way: The majority of stuff you're about to read in this section came from Os Guinness's book *Steering Through Chaos* (Colorado Springs, CO: NavPress Publishing Group, 2000). I had to read it. You should avoid it, though.

Pride as defined above is a foundational sack of cement for the DDP. It is a piece of cake to take on board, as we live in a time in which the deadly sin of pride has actually been twisted into a virtue. Today, we hear that we should love ourselves, pet ourselves and stroke ourselves because we are truly, truly special and can do no wrong. Aren't we the little self-obsessed me-monkeys? Now let's all go back to staring into our belly buttons and not let anyone disturb us.

Arrogance manifests in an inflated sense of self-worth, a peacock-like pre-occupation with self-esteem, an extravagant sense of self-love that makes Narcissus look like a flagellant monk, the notion that we are the most important people on the planet, an arrogant illusion of invulnerability, a claim to the right to our views regardless of reality, and a lack of consideration for the selfishness of others. All of this is an essential part of the dilator's devilish diet.

If the above describes you, well then, you can breathe a big sigh of relief because you have the bellicose bouillabaisse for certain destruction. Rock on, man.

2. Envy
Primal in its poison, envy forms a big chunk of the foul compost heap that stimulates the growth for human stupidity aplenty.

Envy, like pride, is an extremely deadly sin that doesn't get the verbal hailstorm the other sins get in our current culture. Unlike the corporate executive found guilty of "nudging" the numbers a bit, someone who's been saddled by envy will probably not make the evening news. No, envy is not that sexy, and it doesn't get the buzz that zings around a loudmouthed politician, a gay priest or a greedy Enron exec.

Because this sin doesn't get the *National Enquirer*'s attention like the more juicy transgressions, we might tend to see it as less naughty. But be not deceived, my DDP brethren; this sin is a double-meat whopper of deft disaster once it sticks its talons into a person.

Another distinguishing feature about the funk of envy is that it is not all that fun to commit. Envy is the one sin people never like or admit they have. You'll never see someone who is envious chilling out, laughing his butt off or relaxing with his homies while this demon is in the house. The more envy grows, the more it drives its impenitent coddler insane. Of course, it is for this very reason that envy shouldn't be shelved: It is a very effective defective principle that can help people realize their goal of making their lives a living hell.

So, what is envy? I'll start with what it is not. Envy is not admiring what someone else has and wanting some good stuff as well. Envy differs from admiration or emulation in that envy is, as Thomas Aquinas said, "sorrow at another's good." Someone who is centered can watch another person righteously prosper and not hate him or her for it.

Not so for the aspiring DDP. When DDPs see someone else excel, they are slapped in the face with the reality that they just got dogged. But instead of sucking it up and working harder and smarter, they allow their pride to fuel their wounded wittle spirit. This sets dejected DDPs down a path of disparagement of the prosperous that eventually morphs into the desire to destroy the person, party or nation that has just trumped them. Envy is sa-weet, no?

3. Anger
Anger is the third of the seven lethal peccadilloes you should love if you like courting major losses. Anger is a no-duh obvious and brutal vice. When this sin has a hold of your short and curlies, you won't be able to hide it like you can pride or envy or addiction. This offense, as Madonna would say, wants to "express itself." When it does, the person saddled with this slop, those whom it's unleashed on and the general populace that is unfortunate enough to be standing by this bunk will all pay retail for someone's wrath. DDP-perfect. This sin destroys you and harms others. What a perk.

Now, when I talk about the deadliness of anger, indignation, rage, wrath, whatever you want to call it, I'm not talking about the natural ebb and flow of emotions. Heating up is not always evil or deadly.

Anger only turns ugly when it latches onto to the will. And this is what you, the DDP, gotta have to get the full effect of this nastiness. Os Guinness says that "anger becomes a deadly sin . . . when the will is directly responsible for the rise and expression of the emotion." Where people start going over to the dark side with anger is when they intentionally incite and direct unjust indignation with the goal of marking their opponents for destruction.

Anger enables DDPs to blow through the roadblocks of the love of God, the love of one's neighbor and the good sense of their brain. When wrath hits this boiling point, it becomes too powerful for them to control, and it is there that the ramifications become rancid. Can you say, "yummy destruction aplenty"?

4. Sloth

Fourth on the seven deadly sins list is listlessness, or acedia, or spiritual dejection, or sloth, or blah blah . . . whatever. I really don't care anymore. Hey, what time does the *Surreal Life* air on the All-Hope-Is-Gone channel?

Anyway, sloth is essentially the desire to sit on your butt and pick boogers because you're a jaded and dejected bleak little hamster. Sloth is the sin, according to Dorothy Sayers, "which believes nothing, cares for nothing, seeks to know nothing, interferes with nothing, enjoys nothing, loves nothing, hates nothing, finds purpose in nothing, lives for nothing, and only remains alive because there is nothing it will die for."

The decadent tub of spiritual lard that's satiated with this swill will not lift a finger to fight insanity or to stand for God and humanity because, for them, there isn't anything worth getting riled up about. I smell DDP all over this vice. Do you?

As the slothful see it, life has tanked, does tank and will continue to tank, and there's nada they can do about it. Don't ask or expect them to cheerlead any cause, because the world, according to this gloomy group, is irrevocably irreparable.

The sin of sloth, unlike pride, envy, anger, avarice, lust and gluttony, is a sin of omission rather than of commission. Being a sluggard is a simple sin in that all you have to do to do this doo-doo is do nothing when you're s'posed to do something.

When most folks think of someone who's given to sloth, they usually conjure up an image of some bloated, slow moving, mumbling, unshorn, unemployed human sea cow with excessive eye crustations. But the fact is that most indolents aren't your typical heel draggin' slackers.

True slothfulness is easy to hide under a flurry of inconsequential activities and frothy busyness. Yes, you can be hectic, fit, religious and industrious and still be slothful. "But how?" you might ask. Well, here's the real acid test to gauge whether or not you have this soul disease: When that which is consequential confronts you—such as the pursuit of God, the good, the true and the beautiful—how do you react?

Does that which is holy, just and good get a rise out of you and cause you to get off your rear and move into action? Hopefully not, if you aspire to be a DDP. Those who want to embrace this vice must simply stare at the substantial like a calf looking at a new gate and with a shrug of their shoulders say, "Whatever."

Sloth cannot be simply deduced to just loitering in life. Classically defined, sloth is a sluggishness of spirit that is the byproduct of a Van Gogh-esque spiritual gloominess that no longer sees the worthiness of the worthwhile. Ironically, sloth leaves one, as Os Guinness states, trying to find "meaning in its own meaninglessness."

Slothfulness, one more time, is careless apathy toward ideals that leads to a lethargic approach toward that which really matters in life. Ideal for the DDP!

5. Greed

The fifth tool Satan uses to suck DDP suckers into hell is the deadly vice of avarice. Y'know what I'm talking about here, don't 'cha? That "show me the money and I'll sell my soul and my grandmother, become a corporate slug, pimp my integrity, blow off my family, shave my head and walk backward and do whatever to whomever to get my greedy palms on some major cash" attitude.

This sin is so bad in God's eyes and drives so many people and nations into the pit that God had to slap a commandment (the tenth one) forbidding its presence on His planet. But like the rest of God's advice on what to do and not do, if you want to be truly defective, you should blow off His counsel regarding this temptation like E.D. Hill would Carrot Top's amorous advances.

So, what is greed, and why is it such a God-awful awfully good lifestyle choice for the DDP? Greed, as Os Guinness states, "is a sin with two components: getting what we do not have and keeping what we do."

How do you know if greed has got a hold on you? Well, one way to gauge whether or not you're a goner in this arena is how you react when you see a starving kid on television. If it makes you hungry and prompts you to buy another fridge and then go to Costco to fill it, greed's got you. Another indicator that might tip you off that you have officially lost your mind is if you get excited when you read *Money* magazine or watch *Cashin' In* on Fox.

No, greed cannot be deduced to just having or wanting things. Neither can it be simplified by the old stereotype of some money-hoarding, parsimonious spendthrift who can pinch a penny so hard he can make it squeal. No, the soul of this sin, in the words of Guinness, "is not the love of possessions but of possessing and therefore being a possessor." What's ironic about this unmistakable mistake, as Os again states, is that "those who have as their passion the pursuit of possessing end up getting possessed."

This is what you, the DDP, should hope for—namely, getting possessed with greed.

6. Gluttony

Thanks to the pervasive spread of gluttony within the United States, Sherman Klump is no longer just a character in an Eddie Murphy flick . . . chances are, he's you.

Never in American history have there been so many sweaty sea-cow-like adults and so many little chunky-cheese, diseased-primed boys and girls. What's that I smell? I think it's destruction.

I'm 44 years old as I write this closer. When I was 12 years old growing up in Texas, there was only one over-weight kid in my sixth-grade class of 300. That was one boy—not two, not 60 percent of my classmates carting around junk in their trunk—just one. Today, according to MSN online, over half of the adults in the good old U.S. of Excess are overweight, and nearly a quarter of our kids aren't just a little pudgy, they're obese. Wow. DDP paradise.

Just yesterday while I was kayaking in the Atlantic, I saw this one boy (somewhere between 6 to 8 years old) on a boat with his shirt off. This kid was so chubby you could have hidden small toys in the folds of his fat.

Gluttony, according to Os Guinness, is the "idoliza-tion of food." Os states, "Just as avarice idolizes posses-sions and lust sex, so gluttony idolizes food. It lifts it out of its place and distorts both food and eating. Thus, unlike a gourmet who enjoys and appreciates food, a tra-ditional glutton enjoys eating, almost regardless of its taste, beauty or the company shared. Whereas the gour-met savors, the traditional glutton devours."

Now, granted, in the grand scheme of things, gluttony is less egregious than some sins. I would rather be sharing the road with a guy who's had eight hot dogs than a Mel Gibson lit up on eight Glenlivets. Having said that, gluttony remains a delicious DDP sin. Can you say, "delicious"?

Before all you svelte DDP health freaks start to worry that your obsession with fitness will disallow you from the ability to be a glutton, never fear. The medieval view of this vice was not simply constrained to ravenous appetites and bulging hips. That's way too easy and lets far too many food fanatics off the hook. No, the medieval ones saw five ways in which one could maintain the sin of gluttony without looking like a manatee: (1) by eating and drinking too soon, (2) by eating and drinking too expensively, (3) by eating and drinking too much, (4) by eating and drinking too eagerly, and (4) by eating and drinking with too much fuss.

Guinness states that each of these five ways "are all symptoms of a philosophy of life that is finally materialistic, and hedonistic, captured in the motto, 'let us eat and drink, for tomorrow we die.' Thus modern ethicists point out: modern gluttony is not observed only in bulging midriffs, high blood pressures, poisoned livers, bottlenoses and bad breath. It can also be traced in the fanatical modern devotion to dieting, health foods, and drug taking. In a society in which cookbooks outsell the Bible by something like ten to one, food and diets have been given a time and a place that are gluttonous." Worship food, DDP. Worship it! Yee haw!

7. Lust

Lust is the last vice on the Seven Deadly Sins list, and one that has got a hold on our culture's naughty bits. Even Stevie Wonder can see that. We've got a bazillion-dollar Internet and terrestrial porn industry. Our nation's got tribes of teenage boys and girls raised on Lindsay Lohan, Britney Spears and MySpace.com who are more sexually savvy than sailors were 20 years ago. DDP paradise!

Older people are buying into the cult of sexual pleasure as well. Old women who should be growing old with dignity and grace are instead donning mini skirts to show off their beef-jerky-like legs and having tetherballs crammed into their chest in a desperate attempt to relive their college days. Here's a tip for you grandmothers out there: Don't wear a mini-skirt if you are also wearing Depends. And here's some advice for you old guys: If you have a flabby chest, as Dennis Miller says, don't wear tight T-shirts—it confuses the children.

For the aspiring DDP who wishes to embrace the vice of lust, you must believe the greatly exaggerated notion that you'll find nirvana through sex. You need to believe what the prophets of porn tell you when they say you will forever be fulfilled when you zealously pursue your erotic passions. It's salvation through sex for the DDP. So leap on the lust bandwagon like a dog jumps on a June bug. Celebrate the sheer exuberance of the animal spirit. Why shouldn't you? You're cosmically bored and discontent.

Allow yourself to be wooed by Madison Avenue and get irresponsibly wacky with your wedding tackle. Thank the marketers for failing to mention that there is often lasting negative and/or traumatic emotional consequences for illicit sex, that herpes and Chlamydia don't make one happy and clappy, that abortion ain't no picnic, that teenage pregnancies are usually a ticket to poverty, and that wholesome people typically won't want to marry the over-used sexual village bicycle that you now have foolishly become.

Yes, you owe a big debt of gratitude to all the advertisers out there for not telling the truth about the hazards of turning one's body into an amusement park. Thank you, marketers. Thank you for selling us decidedly defective habits.

POSTSCRIPT

WHAT TO DO IF YOU
UNFORTUNATELY SUCCEED

As much as I have prepared you to fail miserably in life,
I know that some of you will still slip through the cracks
and succeed. So, to keep your head from getting wacky
when you start getting rewarded by life, you, the DDP, must
have the following non-negotiable attitudes settled deeply
within you. These five commandments will keep you from
getting all positive and weird should prosperity come.

1. Thou Shalt Be a Jerk

Determine now that you will become a real toad once
you're living in your newly attained prosperity. Let success completely ruin you. I'm sure you have seen this
before . . . once someone achieves something great or
finally gets a little notoriety after years of hard work, he
ends up dumping his spouse, starts neglecting his kids,
discards his true friends and begins to develop a wicked
attitude. This is good.

Some of the positive DDP telltale signs that you're
becoming a jerk include the following:

- You speak about yourself in the third person. (People who do this almost never recover from their narcissistic nightmare.)
- You begin to believe people when they tell you how great you are, which inevitably leads you to think you can get away with murder.
- You start demanding Evian, and *only* Evian.
- You become extremely picky about the food you'll eat.
- You begin to lose your high-quality friends and start attracting human hyenas from hell.

One thing that you must do is embrace pride and arrogance, because pride goes before destruction and a haughty spirit goes before a fall. To help destroy yourself and make certain you do a face plant into the concrete after you succeed, stay conceited. Your loftiness will make people repulsed at the mere mention of your name.

2. Thou Shalt Gloat Over Thine Enemies

Another way to slay yourself and stoop to new pathetic levels is to gloat over your enemies when your accomplishment arrives. Try to acquire an abundance of enemies and then blindly revel in your accomplishments and their pathetic lack. This will make you loathsome, blind you to your own frailties and set you up to come crashing down with no one to pick you up.

Return evil for evil and insult for insult. Exact vengeance on people and turn into a bitter and spiteful crank that heaps scorn on people who have wronged you. This spirit will wither you from the inside out and cause you to lack enjoyment in all that you have achieved.

If people have wronged you, ridiculed you or criticized you, do not blow it off and just walk away. Spend your energy getting yourself tied up in their words and their warped little worlds. Do not move on or move up. When you succeed, rub their noses in it and tell them, "I told you so." As a matter of fact, go the next mile and curse your enemies.

Trust me, if you do this, your prosperity will be on its way out the door once this madness begins to take hold of you. Isn't that cool?

3. Thou Shalt Sit on Thine Butt Praising Thyself

Hey, man, enjoy your success and congratulate yourself on your accomplishments. Worship what you've done. You'll start getting fat. You'll start thinking that nothing can go wrong and that you'll always be at the top of the world looking down on creation. Get deluded, dude.

Become passive and self-obsessed. Sit around for long periods of time looking in the mirror and telling yourself how pretty and how great you are. Don't look for the next battle or the next obstacle to conquer. Don't be cautious about taking too long of a break between your achievements. This *laissez faire* attitude is most excellent in clothes-lining you should you find success.

Get it into your mind that success is just a matter of getting more money and that there's nothing greater in this world than getting a bunch of cash. Seek to praise yourself. Be pleased with the wealth and possessions you've accumulated and don't strive to become a purpose-driven person. If you want to be a DDP but find yourself succeeding in life, you can make that success short-lived if you become a soul-stroking, self-pleasuring individual.

Rest on your laurels after you get what you're after. After attaining your goal, do not move on to the next challenge. Rather, set an altar around an award you've won and worship it. That's what pathetic people do. Prolong your enjoyment of your current accomplishment, as this will keep you from future greatness.

4. Thou Shalt Worship Material Stuff

Worshiping this world's goods is not a sin. What does God know? Matter of fact, you should let your heart get attached to the treasures your efforts have afforded you—you know, things like better food, better cars, nicer houses, and such. These items need to become your priority and focus, not people, ideas and serving your fellow man. Puh-lease!

In order to keep your heart materialistic, keep the following in mind:

- The Beatles lied when they sang, "Money can't buy me love." It can buy you lots of stuff. For the guys, it can buy you a bunch of dumb chicks; for the girls, it can buy you tons of flaky guys that will treat you like dirt. It can attract low-life moochers and opportunists. It might not buy you love, but it can buy you fun. And that's pretty close.

- Money and material possessions can be here today and gone tomorrow. Therefore, you should go nuts and abuse what you have, because according to your art teacher, there is no afterlife. This is all that there is.

So, my rich little buddy, use your cash, spend your cash, enjoy your cash, and understand that money is everything. If handled incorrectly, money can cause not only great pain but also pummel people and sink them in inordinate affections.

5. Thou Shalt Forget Others Who Helped Thee

When people are struggling to get something they are after, they always pray to God and lean heavily on the counsel and capital of others. If you do this, here's what you must do to destroy whatever you've accomplished: When success manifests, quickly blow off God and man and start living and acting as if you did it all on your own.

My little DDP buddy, the opportunity to act like a jerk and pretend you obtained all this stuff on your own will move you to ingratitude and arrogance. When you feel this impulse, jump on it and milk it for everything its worth. After life starts paying you back in spades and you feel compelled to thank God and your friends, determine to change into an egotistical monster who completely snubs his support base. Very nice. This is what you want to become: jaded and forgetful of other people's and God's assistance.

Let your prayer life begin to vaporize. Become real selfish. Start preening like never before. A true DDP will not avoid becoming ungrateful once the God of heaven has answered his or her prayers. Do not continue to pray, hold fast to your convictions or love what is right and true. Instead, start acting like a spoiled me-monkey.

In addition, you must also overlook your friends, family, teachers and tutors who helped you to get where you are right now in life through education, exhortation, encouragement and intercession. Become absolutely ungrateful toward these people. A real DDP only stays true to his or her friends in the rain, never in the sun.

* * *

Whew, I feel as if I have just delivered what's left of my soul to you. I HAVE NOTHING LEFT. Yet if I were to die today, I would die knowing that I did all I could to awaken the inner wuss within the losing DDP whiners of my generation. I have labored sorta arduously to supply you with these 10 habits of decidedly defective people and have tossed you a substantial bone by outlining vices guaranteed to get God even more ticked off at you. I can do no more but hope, wish and pray that you don't change your course, depart from these debilitating principles and iniquities, and end up getting a life.

AN ADDENDUM FOR THE NDDP (NON-DECIDEDLY DEFECTIVE PERSON)

My goofy editors wanted me to write something to the NDDP. What a pain. It's not like NDDPs need more motivation—they already get the lion's share of attention from other authors. The NDDP are the Marcia Bradys of the publishing world. Marcia, Marcia, Marcia. It's all about Marcia.

I've had it with being inspirational. I'm trying to help DDPs destroy their lives. Why can't my publisher see that this is counterintuitive to where I'm trying to drive my herd?

Y'know, the only reason why I am going to go along with this is because if I don't I won't get paid, and since I'm trying to become greedy and fall in love with money (a deadly sin!), I'll capitulate with some crumbs for those who want an effective life. But you're not going to get much out of me. Matter of fact, I think I'll just rehash some of my stuff from my book *The Bulldog Attitude: Get It or Get Left Behind.* That way I can please my editors and nurture my slothful spirit as I keep on the path of least resistance.

So, at gunpoint of my publisher, I offer the following pointers to those who don't like the certain demise of

DDPs and want to steer clear of forever sitting on their rear. These tips will provide you with a quick start to guide your life away from the quicksand of misery. Giddy up.

1. Figure Out What Motivates You

One way to move away from an existence that stinks, as Dennis Millers says, "worse than an airplane toilet," is to find your groove. What flicks your switch? If you could do whatever you wanted and it was righteous and somewhat feasible, what would you do? You have to define your passion.

Take the time to figure out what stirs your heart. Pinpoint it. Write it down. Now go out and do it. Don't play around. Winners aren't indecisive DDPs. NDDPs don't float from being philosophers to army men to secret agents to brain surgeons. They know exactly what they want and won't settle for anything else.

NDDPs might have a few side interests, but they jam to a solid, funky, bottom-line bass note that is clear and unchanging. NDDPs are able to spit out with absolute clarity what they are about, what they will live for and what they want from life—in their personal life, family life and vocational life. So to be successful, define what you want, when you want it and in what quantity. If you don't, you will be a woulda-shoulda-coulda DDP the rest of your life.

2. Pull the Plug on the TV

Second, you must cut the fat. By "fat," I mean all the excess baggage, activities and slop that are detrimental to your future progress. A good place to start is by cutting out TV. If you want to truly succeed in life, you need to get this into your brain: Television is an "EIR," an electronic income reducer. TV has killed more dreams and visions than crack could ever hope to do.

If you watch TV, let it serve you instead of your serving it. Watch selectively. Watch shows that push you to greatness. Watch what is noble and beneficial. In other words, turn the dang thing off. Use your time wisely. If you lose your money, you can get it back; if you lose your time, it's gone for good.

Imagine what an incredible person you could be if instead of watching TV you utilized your time developing your gifts, spending time with your kids, loving on your spouse or just chillin' with energetic butt-kickin' peers and mentors.

3. Change Your Crowd

To avoid the demise that will inevitably occur to all DDPs, you will also need to cut out all of your nonproductive relationships. Dad, quit hanging around with your dip-stick buddies who resemble the cast of *King of the Hill*. Find people who challenge you. Mom, don't let a gossip-ing, messed-up, sexless, desperately-needs-to-get-a-life, soap-opera-watching devotee eternally tie up your phone line or life.

Young person, don't hang out with Satan-worshiping punks who wear Che Guevara T-shirts and have so many body piercings they look like a tackle box blew up in their face. You must also get away from kids who are always walking around holding their crotches, calling girls "hos" and "bitches," and who only use their heads to house dope smoke. You must flee the DDP if you want to be a NDDP.

Look, I'm not trying to be ugly. I firmly believe in loving your neighbor, but I think it is critical that you choose your neighborhood. If you want to pimp your life, you've got to change your crowd. Since some of your friends and family members could be your greatest hindrances, you might have to make new relationships. But even if you don't have to end many of your current relationships (which would be odd), you should at least make yourself add to the reper-toire of the people who can positively affect your life.

You will experience radical growth by simply hanging out with new people who are committed to excellence.

Sure, initially it will be uncomfortable, but it's not near as uncomfortable as the pain that comes through getting your butt kicked by hanging out with idiots.

4. Set Challenging Goals

If you want to soar in life, you've got to set killer goals. Outrageous, hard-to-reach targets will motivate you far more than reasonable ones. Never pick a small fight. In the Bible, David challenged and killed Goliath, not Goliath's ugly sister. What kind of a challenge would it be for a pit bull to whip a toy poodle?

You've got to set goals for yourself that will stretch you like a water-ski rope with a fat kid at the other end of it. Never measure your vision by what is reachable or by what other people are doing, but always go for "mission impossible." Incite people's ridicule and use their derision to spur you to greatness. Your success will be the sweetest revenge.

5. Never Give Up or Look Back

Finally, you must tattoo these words on your soul: "I will not quit." If you find that you are not in the sweet spot of life that you'd like to be in, you need to have the attitude of a bulldog to get yourself there. You need tenacity. As my blood brother Ted Nugent said, you've got to live "tooth, fang and claw." If you want to be different from the DDP, you've got to be scrappy and plow through whatever you have to plow through.

One more word: If you have really blown it in the past, suck it up and move forward. Don't let your past kill your newfound attitude. Take a good look over your right shoulder . . . then your left . . . and make that the last time you ever look back. From now on, you are an NDDP. Damn the torpedoes. Live all out. And more than likely . . . we'll see you at the top.

ABOUT THE AUTHOR

Doug Giles, despite his best efforts at self destruction, is a popular columnist (Townhall.com, the nation's largest conservative news portal), author, TV and radio personality, minister, hunting and fishing fanatic, and the author of this book, *10 Habits of Decidedly Defective People.*

Giles's writings and his audio ramblings at Clash Radio.com have won several national and international awards, which he says "must be a sign that Armageddon is just around the corner."

Doug, his wife, Mary Margaret, and his two teenage daughters live in a tent and smoke cigars on Tuesday and Thursday evenings around 5:30 or 6:00. Their GPS coordinates are: Latitude 26° 05′ 00″ N. Longitude 80° 46′ 12″ W.

Oh yeah, they also have a dog named Spunky that speaks English and Spanish and teaches T'ai Chi every Wednesday and Friday mornings to angry and disenfranchised nuns in an undisclosed alley behind a Wal-Mart in Florida.

Please send all questions and comments regarding this book to
www.thatchapterwassupposedtobeblankyouidiot.com.
If that doesn't work, try mail@clashradio.com or mail your
comments to P.O. Box 800554, Aventura, FL 33280.

What Lies Did You Tell Today?

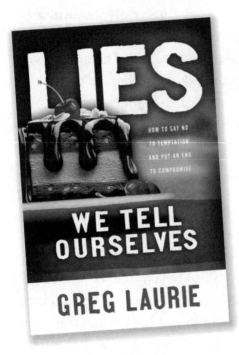

Lies We Tell Ourselves
*How to Say No to Temptation and Put
an End to Compromise*
Greg Laurie
ISBN 978.08307.42752

*I know it's wrong…but every-
body is doing it.
I'll quit tomorrow.
It's not my fault!
I can't help it; I've been under
so much stress…
I deserve this.*

Sound familiar? We often tell
a little white lie and then wonder why we were tempted to
do something wrong. We
don't recognize that the lies
we tell ourselves often lead to
sinful behavior.

Here, dynamic pastor Greg
Laurie takes an honest and
often humorous look at the
ways we fall into sin and how
we frequently rationalize our
actions. Drawing from the
pages of Scriptures and his
own experiences, he shares
practical steps you can take to
effectively resist temptation
and put an end to the com-
promises that will ultimately
harm you. Discover how
telling the truth will change
your life!